THE INS AND OUTS OF CAT CARRIERS:
A VETERINARIAN'S GUIDE TO CAT CARRIERS

WRITTEN AND ILLUSTRATED BY
DR. MANSUM YAU

AVM Services
Vancouver, Canada

AVM Services

DR. MANSUM

Dr. Mansum Yau
www.drmansum.com
@drmansum

Edited by Liisa Salo
Proofread by Arlene Prunkl
Indexed by Mansum Yau
Design and layout by jellyfishdesign.com
Illustrations by Mansum Yau
Author portrait photography by John Bello, Haus of Rufus

1. PETS / Cats / General 2. PETS / Reference 3. TRAVEL / Special Interest / Pets

First Edition: 2024
Updated First Edition: 2025

This edition includes minor updates and additional content not present in the original 2024 release.

ISBN (eBook): 978-1-7383837-1-9
ISBN (Paperback): 978-1-7383837-0-2

This book was written for the purpose of preventive health, was not sponsored, and does not replace the advice of your veterinarian. Consult your veterinarian before giving any medications or supplements.

To a cat who gives the best hugs,
eagerly waits by the door, and loves forests:

BOO BEAR YAU

TABLE OF CONTENTS

LETTER FROM THE AUTHOR

Dear Cat Lover,

Thank you for picking up this book. Yes, this entire book is about cat carriers. I didn't know I could write so many pages on one topic. I'm glad I did, though, because there's not enough info or awareness about cat carriers.

Since graduating from vet school in 2010, I've seen so many cat owners and veterinary staff struggling with carriers: struggling to get cats in, struggling to get cats out, struggling to take carriers apart, struggling to put them back together. Sometimes cats don't show up for appointments when they're sick or injured because their owners can't get them into their carriers. I remember thinking it doesn't have to be this way and wishing there was a way I could help. Voila, a book on the ins and outs of cat carriers!

I didn't want this book to be like the info that you can find online. I wanted it to be both informative and fun to read, like a magazine. Except instead of ads, there are cartoons and affirmations.

I hope this book becomes a favorite you'll want to revisit, offering a pick-me-up during stressful times and a welcome addition to your coffee table. You can read it from cover to cover or jump from one section to another.

There are helpful tips on how to get your cat into and out of a carrier and on how to pick the right type of carrier for you and your cat, plus fun quizzes, horoscopes, a guided meditation to calm your nerves before using a carrier, and much more! There's even an interview with Starry, a cartoon cat I dreamed up.

I've dreamed of being an author and illustrator since I was a kid, so this book is a dream come true. It wasn't easy finding the time and energy to write and draw after work as a full-time vet, but I'm very glad I did. I hope you enjoy reading this book as much as I enjoyed writing and illustrating it.

Paws and whiskers,

Dr. Mansum Yau
Ontario Veterinary College Class of 2010
Cat Friendly, Human-Animal Bond, and
Fear-Free Certified

DR. MANSUM YAU'S LIST OF ESSENTIAL SUPPLIES FOR CATS

- ☐ Food, food puzzles, and bowls
- ☐ Water, water fountain, and bowls
- ☐ Scratching posts, cat trees, and toys
- ☐ Nail trimmers, combs, and brushes
- ☐ Toothbrushes and toothpaste
- ☐ Cone collars
- ☐ Litter boxes and litter
- ☐ Cat carriers

Yes, the cat carrier is an essential item for cats. A carrier needs to be used any time a cat needs to be transported. Being able to get your cat into and out of a carrier is an important skill if you have a cat. I'm not just saying this because I'm a vet who wants you to be able to take your cats to the vet when they're ill or injured. I'm saying this as a vet who loves cats and wants the best for them.

Cat carriers should be used in the following situations:

1. Vet visits
2. Grooming appointments
3. Emergencies such as house fires, wildfires, earthquakes, floods, landslides, hurricanes, tornadoes, tsunamis, and military invasions when evacuation is necessary
4. Moving
5. Vacations
6. Adventures outside the home such as hiking, camping, etc.
7. A safe place at home for your cat to sleep or to hide in when scared, anxious, or stressed

Here are some reasons why cat carriers should be used:

1. To prevent your cat from escaping and getting lost, hit by a car, etc.
2. To prevent other animals from attacking your cat and vice versa
3. To provide protection during collisions
4. To prevent collisions caused by your cat distracting you while driving
5. To prevent your cat from biting or scratching your veterinary team/groomer
6. To be able to fly your cat on a plane or use public transportation
7. To provide a sanctuary for your cat to sleep and hide in when scared, anxious, or stressed

This list might sound repetitive or common sense, but some cat people genuinely aren't aware of some of these reasons for using carriers.

CAT CARRIERS 101

Never discipline your cat by confining them in a carrier. Doing so could make your cat dislike or fear the carrier.

TAKE-HOME MESSAGE

Even if it's hard to get your cat into the carrier, it's important to use one to transport your cat. If you don't use a carrier, you can put your cat, yourself, other drivers in the parking lot or on the road, and your veterinary staff or groomer at risk. Please don't hand your cat over to a veterinary team member or groomer without a carrier, especially when outside in a parking lot or on the curb.

A cat carrier is as important as a:

1. Helmet
2. Seat belt
3. Child car seat, also known as (AKA) infant seat, child seat, car seat, or booster seat
4. Kennel or crate for a dog

Many people kennel train their dogs when they first take them home. Many people don't carrier train their cats. They shove their cat into a carrier, have the cat panicking in the carrier, and then expect their vet to deal with the cat that's fighting tooth and nail (pun intended). There needs to be a shift in mentality regarding cats and their carriers. Cats can be trained, and they can benefit from the safety and comfort of their carriers too.

For more info on carrier training, see page 23.

Here are some benefits of having a carrier-trained cat:

1. Fewer injuries to the cat, cat owner, groomer, and/or veterinary staff
2. Reduced stress for the cat in the carrier
3. Reduced stress during car rides and vet exams (Pratsch et al., 64)
4. Reduced stress for the cat owner
5. Increased ability to take your cat to the vet or groomer (fewer no-show appointments)

Why can it be hard to get a cat into and/or out of a carrier?

1. Your cat can be scared of new things like the carrier (neophobic).
2. Your cat might have had negative experiences in the carrier in the past.
3. Your carrier might not be designed for easy cat entry or exit.
4. Cats have sharp teeth and claws.
5. Cats can contort their bodies like gymnasts.
6. You haven't learned any tips and tricks for getting a cat into a carrier.
7. Physical limitations of the owner such as arthritis can make it challenging to handle the carrier and the cat.

IT DOESN'T HAVE TO BE HARD!

This book will give you tips and tricks for getting cats into and out of carriers. It'll help you and your cat see carriers in ways you haven't before.

Cat, meet Carrier

THE CARRIER DOESN'T HAVE TO BE SCARY LIKE A MONSTER OR A DOG.

Some cats think:

Carrier = visit to vet
= poking, prodding, and pain
(negative experience)

We can train cats to think:

Carrier = safe place
(positive experience)

Carrier = treats
(positive experience)

Carrier = adventure
(positive experience)

Less stress in carrier

potentially = less stress in vet clinic

If your cat does any of the following in a carrier:

- Open-mouth breathing
- Constant, loud vocalization the whole trip
- Fearful urination and/or defecation
- Frantic attempts to escape the carrier, leading to broken nails, etc.
- Aggression, biting, and swatting at humans

Ask your vet about gabapentin, a calming medication or pre-visit pharmaceutical that your cat can take at home before using a carrier, just like some people have to take a calming medication before they go to the dentist.

TAKE-HOME MESSAGE

Ask your vet about gabapentin if your cat gets overly stressed in the carrier.

Getting cats out of carriers is generally easier than getting them in. However, there are cats that won't come out once they reach the vet's office. They might be anxious about what awaits them once they leave the carrier.

A lot of cat owners don't think about how hard it can be for veterinary staff to get cats out of carriers. There's the risk of getting bitten or scratched. To prevent injuries and to prevent forceful handling of cats (pulling or dumping cats out), veterinary staff often have to take carriers apart to get cats out gently and safely.

Some cat carriers aren't designed to be taken apart easily. There can be a lot of screws or pegs to remove. There can also be things hindering the carriers from being taken apart like rusty screws and zip ties, AKA cable ties or zap straps. Rusty screws and zip ties can break, leading to your carrier falling apart and endangering your cat.

TAKE-HOME MESSAGE

Please replace your carrier if:

1) There are screws or parts missing. Please don't use zip ties.

2) There are rusty screws.

Before this book was written, the only statistics available on cat carriers were expensive market statistics. There were no statistics available on carriers from vet clinics. What type of cat carriers do veterinary professionals prefer? What percentage of cat owners find it hard to put cats into carriers? What's the most common type of cat carrier used?

I set out to find statistics by surveying both veterinary professionals and cat owners, as well as by keeping a tally (results on page 47). This was my first foray into the land of surveys, so statisticians, please don't judge them too harshly.

To see the surveys, see pages 104-106.

CAT CARRIER STATISTICS

SURVEYING CAT OWNERS

IN-CLINIC PAPER SURVEY

The first survey I conducted was completed by cat owners and distributed during their appointments with their cats at seven different Canadian vet clinics where I was a locum or relief vet. These appointments were booked by receptionists, not by me, with cats of random ages and breeds. A total of 119 surveys were taken in six months from January 1 to June 30, 2022.

This survey had three closed-ended questions and one open-ended question:

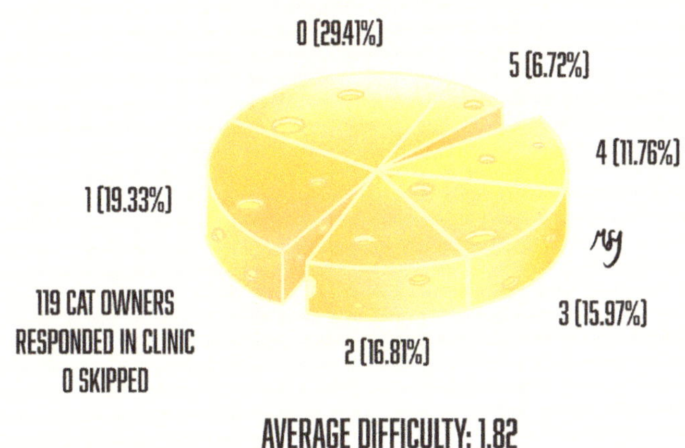

1 **Please rate how difficult you find putting your cat into a carrier (from 0 to 5, 0 being very easy and 5 being a nightmare).**

The average difficulty was 1.82. In other words, the average cat owner who took this survey in-clinic didn't find putting their cat into a carrier difficult. One drawback of this survey question is the reliance on subjective ratings. What one person finds easy might be difficult for another person.

People who struggle to get their cat into a carrier might have missed their appointments and, consequently, did not participate in this survey. No-shows or cancellations = no survey taken.

PLEASE RATE HOW DIFFICULT YOU FIND TAKING YOUR CAT OUT OF A CARRIER AT THE VET.

(0: EASY PEASY, 5: NIGHTMARE)

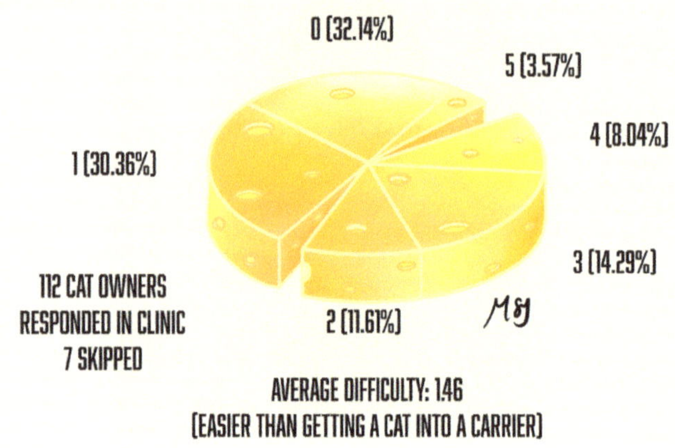

AVERAGE DIFFICULTY: 1.46
(EASIER THAN GETTING A CAT INTO A CARRIER)

2 **Please rate how difficult you find taking your cat out of a carrier at the vet (from 0 to 5).**

This question wasn't applicable during COVID-19 when cat owners couldn't accompany their pets inside many vet clinics (curbside pickup).

3 **Did you know there are more types of cat carriers than just hard-sided or soft-sided carriers? Y/N**

See page 40 for info on the different types of carriers.

The majority of cat owners who took the survey, 53%, didn't know that there are other types of cat carriers. This was reflected in the tally that I took. (See page 47 for more info.) The majority of my feline patients were brought to the vet clinic in soft- or hard-sided non-collapsible handheld carriers as opposed to other types such as backpacks or rolling carriers.

4 **Please share a cat carrier success or horror story if you have one to help other cat parents.**

Instead of sharing stories, most cat owners shared the tip of putting a hard-sided carrier on its side with the door facing the ceiling and lowering a cat in feet first. I'm glad they know this trick for getting cats into hard-sided carriers with only one door.

DID YOU KNOW THERE ARE MORE TYPES OF CAT CARRIERS THAN JUST HARD-SIDED OR SOFT-SIDED CARRIERS?

THE MAJORITY OF CAT OWNERS IN THIS ONLINE SURVEY DIDN'T KNOW ABOUT NON-TRADITIONAL CARRIERS.

ONLINE SURVEY

A total of 262 cat owners around the world filled out this survey on SurveyMonkey. It had six closed-ended questions:

1 **Please rate how difficult you find putting your cat into a carrier (from 1 to 5, 1 being very easy and 5 being a nightmare).**

The average answer was 2.83 (moderately difficult). I was hoping to compare the average answer from this online question to the average answer of the in-clinic paper survey question. Unfortunately, I couldn't because the scale for the online survey (1-5) didn't match the scale for the paper survey (0-5).

Note: I didn't include the question on how hard it is to take cats out of the carrier at the vet as this survey took place during a time when many vet clinics were still doing curbside pickup. Hence most owners weren't present when cats were taken out of carriers at the vet.

I added several questions to the online survey not included in the paper survey:

2 **Would you take your cat to the vet more than you already do if it were easier? Y/N**

As a vet, I wanted to determine if difficulty getting cats into their carriers was preventing owners from seeking more veterinary care. According to this survey, a third of the participants said they would take their cats to the vet more often if it were easier.

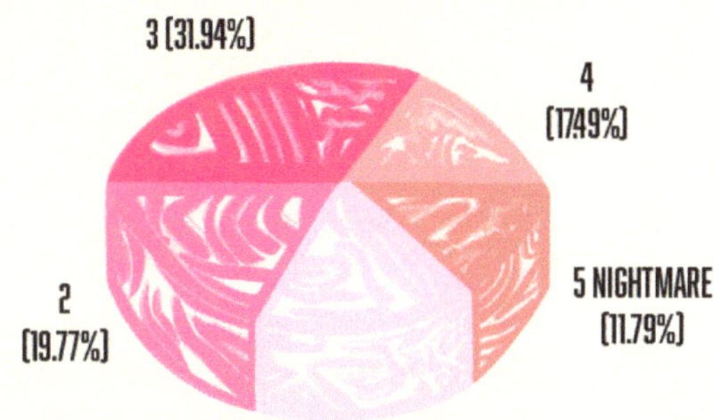

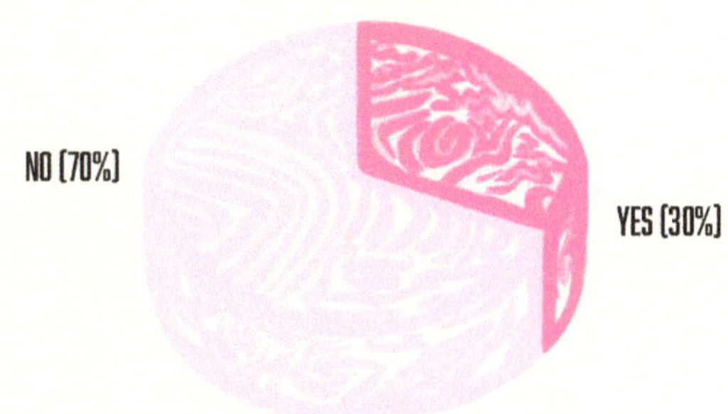

3   Did you know that veterinary staff dislike zip ties, AKA cable ties or zap straps, on cat carriers? Y/N

The majority of cat owners who responded to the survey, 71%, didn't know.

Using zip ties on carriers with missing screws, pegs, and/or clips makes it a lot harder to take cats out of the carrier and a lot more stressful for the cat; e.g., having to dump or pull them out because the zip ties prevent the lid of the carrier from being taken off. Using zip ties can also jeopardize the safety of your cat because they can break.

One anonymous survey participant said that she'd never seen zip ties on carriers before even though she used to work at a vet clinic. I personally have seen them used in multiple North American cities.

See the *Cat Carrier Horror Stories* section on pages 31–33.

4   Did you know veterinary staff dislike rusty screws on cat carriers? Y/N

Fifty-two percent of cat owners who responded to the survey said yes. Just like zip ties, rusty screws can break. They also prevent the lid from being taken off, making it harder to get cats out of carriers and hence more stressful for the cat.

THE MAJORITY OF CAT OWNERS TAKING THIS ONLINE SURVEY KNEW VETERINARY STAFF DISLIKE RUSTY SCREWS ON CAT CARRIERS.

THE MAJORITY OF CAT OWNERS DIDN'T KNOW VETERINARY STAFF DISLIKE ZIP TIES ON CAT CARRIERS.

It makes sense lower-income cat owners would use zip ties to avoid buying a new carrier when screws, pegs, and/or clips are missing. Cat carriers don't have to be expensive, however. See page 39 for tips on where to get inexpensive or even free carriers.

TAKE-HOME MESSAGE

Please replace your carrier if:

1) There are screws or parts missing. Please don't use zip ties.

2) There are rusty screws.

5 Did you know there are more types of cat carriers than just hard-sided or soft-sided carriers? Y/N

More than half of the cat owners who responded to the survey, 58%, said no. Judging by the number of people who've stopped me and my cat to take pictures of him in his backpack, I'm not surprised. There are cat owners who've never seen a cat backpack or rolling carrier before, although they are becoming more popular.

6 Do you wish there were more resources to help you get your cat into a carrier?

Fifty-six percent said yes. Well, I hope this book helps! To my knowledge, this is the only in-depth book on cat carriers with tips on how to get cats into and out of cat carriers, how to know when it's time to replace your cat carrier, how to choose the right type of cat carrier for you and your cat, and much more. Keep reading to learn more!

Note: I didn't ask participants to share a cat carrier success or horror story on the online survey because on the paper survey, most people left it blank or shared tips instead.

Another question I should've asked is: Where do you put your cat carrier when you get home? Is it left out for your cat to sleep in, tucked away in a closet, stored in the attic, or kept in the garage?

DID YOU KNOW THERE ARE MORE TYPES OF CAT CARRIERS THAN JUST HARD-SIDED OR SOFT-SIDED CARRIERS?

THE MAJORITY OF CAT OWNERS IN THIS ONLINE SURVEY DIDN'T KNOW ABOUT NON-TRADITIONAL CARRIERS.

DO YOU WISH THERE WERE MORE RESOURCES TO HELP YOU GET YOUR CAT INTO A CARRIER?

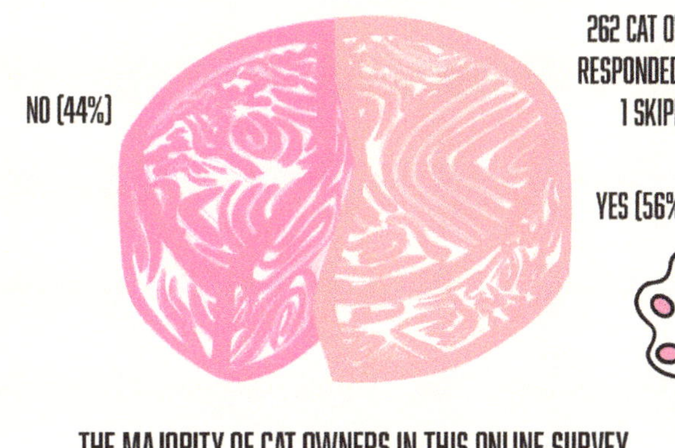

THE MAJORITY OF CAT OWNERS IN THIS ONLINE SURVEY WISHED THERE WERE MORE RESOURCES TO HELP THEM GET THEIR CATS INTO CARRIERS.

SURVEYING VETERINARY PROFESSIONALS

Vets, vet techs AKA vet nurses, and vet assistants around the world filled out a survey either online through SurveyMonkey or on paper. This survey was taken by a total of 247 veterinary professionals in six months from January 1, 2022 to June 30, 2022.

The survey had three questions:

WHAT TYPE OF CARRIER DO YOU FIND THE EASIEST TO TAKE CATS OUT OF?

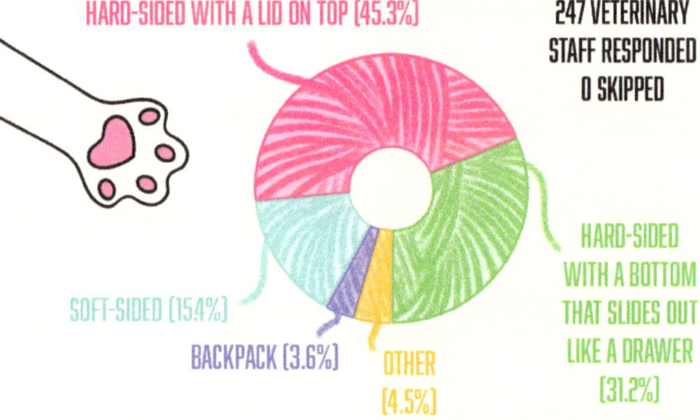

WHAT IS ONE THING YOU WISH MORE CAT OWNERS KNEW ABOUT?

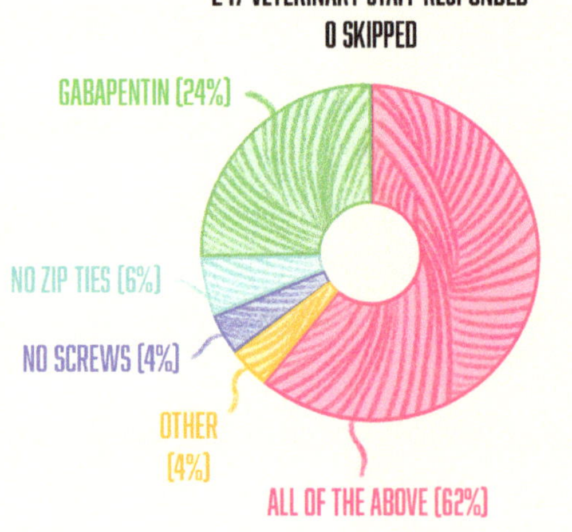

1 At work, what type of carrier do you find the easiest to take cats out of?

The majority, 45%, almost half of the veterinary professionals who took the survey, chose the hard-sided carrier with a lid on top.

Next most popular was the hard-sided carrier with a bottom that slides out like a drawer. That said, some veterinary professionals I spoke to had never seen this time of carrier before because it's a newer design. I wonder if more people would've picked this type of carrier if they were more familiar with it.

TAKE-HOME MESSAGE

The hard-sided carrier with a lid on top is the preferred type of cat carrier of most veterinary professionals (who took this survey).

2 What is one thing you wish more cat parents knew about?

The majority of veterinary professionals, 62%, wished more cat parents knew about gabapentin, a calming medication or pre-visit pharmaceutical that cats can take at home before using a carrier, as well as not having screws or zip ties on cat carriers (or all of the above). Of the three choices, gabapentin is what most veterinary professionals wished more cat parents knew about.

TAKE-HOME MESSAGE

Ask your vet about gabapentin if your cat gets overly stressed in the carrier.

3

Please share a cat carrier success or horror story if you have one to help cat parents.

There was an overwhelming number of horror stories of cats escaping from their carriers outside vet clinics in the parking lot.

See the *Cat Carrier Horror Stories* section on pages 31–33.

Note: A second survey was created and filled out by a small group of 18 veterinary professionals (different from the ones who filled out the other survey). I discontinued this second survey because the answers to the multiple-choice questions were confusing.

To participate in future surveys about pets, please visit **www.drmansum.com**

MAKE IT BIGGER, HUMAN.

CAT CARRIERS IN MOVIES, TV SHOWS, AND CARTOONS

Have you noticed how cat carriers are portrayed in mass media? Cat carriers are often *not* portrayed or used, and even when they are, there's usually only one type: the hard-sided carrier. Mass media doesn't give the audience a realistic or proper idea of how to take pets to the vet. Here's a list of Western movies, TV shows, and cartoons depicting cat carriers, excluding documentaries and reality shows with vets:

MOVIES

NINE LIVES (2016)

A businessman got trapped in the body of his daughter's new Ragdoll cat called Mr. Fuzzypants in this comedy. He got the cat from a mysterious pet store and took him home in a letter box-shaped wicker carrier. This was the only type of cat carrier visible in this small and cluttered pet store.

My analysis: Wicker cat carriers are hard to find nowadays. See page 40 and 111 for more info. Most pet stores sell more than one type of cat carrier. (Even more types are available online.) The main character in this movie showed up to the pet store to get a cat without doing any research on what cats need—please do your research and continue reading this book.

A STREET CAT NAMED BOB (2016)

In this biographical drama movie, a former homeless man named James Bowen took a stray cat that he named Bob to the vet wrapped in a jacket. As he entered the vet clinic, he encountered another man holding a cat without a carrier, not wrapped in anything. Waiting in the reception room of the vet clinic were the following: a rabbit sitting on a lap, two hard-sided cat carriers, and dogs on leashes.

My analysis: Please don't take your cat or rabbit to the vet without a carrier. I understand why James Bowen didn't have a carrier, but what about the other people at the vet? Some cats and dogs have a strong prey drive. Bob the cat could've been attacked by a dog or another cat. The rabbit could've been attacked by cats and dogs.

In the 2012 autobiographical book that this movie is based on, Bowen mentioned he took Bob to the vet in a green, plastic recycling box with the lid resting "loosely on the box." He also mentioned dogs were growling at cats inside their "smart carriers" and "Bob stood out like a sore thumb in his improvised carrier" in the reception room (Bowen, 2012). It's unclear why the movie producers chose to depict the scene differently, especially since the movie is a biographical drama, not a comedy.

THE SECRET LIFE OF PETS 2 (2019)

In this animated movie, a dog was taken to the vet on a leash for scratching. Waiting in the reception room of the vet clinic were the following: a fractious cat wearing a harness but no leash or carrier, a parrot sitting on a lap with no cage, a tortoise sitting on a lap, two cats in one hard-sided carrier, a hamster in a cage, and dogs on leashes.

My analysis: The cat not in a carrier and the parrot could've easily escaped. One or more of the animals could've been attacked. Even if they didn't get attacked, can you imagine how scared they were? Also, the two cats in the same carrier could've gotten into a fight.

MISS AMERICANA (2020)

This documentary showcased singer, songwriter, actress, and cat lover, Taylor Swift. There's a scene with her wearing a brown backpack carrier on a private plane. Her cat Olivia Benson can be seen through the backpack's transparent bubble window.

My analysis: I'm glad Taylor Swift found a carrier that works for her cat, Olivia Benson. She was previously photographed holding Olivia Benson without a carrier walking from a car to her home in New York City. According to an interview with Access Hollywood at the iHeartRadio Music Festival in Las Vegas on September 19, 2014, "[Olivia Benson] freaks out about being put in the cat carrier."

ARGYLLE (2024)

In this spy action movie, the main character had a Scottish Fold cat named Alfie (played by supermodel Claudia Schiffer's cat Chip) that travelled in a backpack carrier with a clear bubble-like window. Promotional posters for the movie featured Alfie in a backpack carrier. Argylle even collaborated with Travel Cat, creating a line of backpack carriers and other cat accessories with the iconic argyle pattern made of diamonds.

My analysis: This movie showed backpack carriers front and centre, not hard-sided carriers. Time will tell if it becomes trendsetting.

Here are movies that should depict cat carriers but don't:

GARFIELD: THE MOVIE (2004)

In this live action/computer-animated movie based on the comic strip created by Jim Davis, Garfield escaped from the vet clinic. He wasn't in a cat carrier, so he was able to run away. Waiting in the reception room of the vet clinic were the following: a monkey sitting on a lap, a snake on a lap, and dogs on leashes.

My analysis of this scene: One or more of the animals could've been attacked without the use of carriers or cages, not to mention Garfield escaped and could've been hit by a car outside the clinic.

CLIFFORD THE BIG RED DOG (2021)

In this live action/computer-animated movie based on a children's book series by Norman Bridwell, a giant red dog named Clifford was taken to the vet. Waiting in the reception room of the vet clinic were the following: dogs on leashes, a chicken on someone's lap not far from a dog, a parrot sitting on another person's lap, and a cat—wait for it—sitting on a lap, not in a carrier.

My analysis: Even though this movie scene was filmed in a real vet clinic, it's highly unlikely to see pet chickens, parrots, cats, and dogs in the same room together in real life. Taking cats and birds to the vet without carriers or cages to prevent them from escaping or getting attacked by (other) cats or by dogs is definitely not recommended.

TV SHOWS

TRAILER PARK BOYS (2001–2007)

This Canadian mockumentary sitcom TV series featured a group of three delinquent men living in a trailer park. One of them was a man named Bubbles, the caretaker of twenty-five-plus stray cats. In one scene, he had to make a trip to the vet after one of the cats got diarrhea from drinking garbage juice. He used a tan-coloured hard-sided carrier with screws to transport the cat. In another scene set in a vet clinic, he got mad at other people for taking his cats to the vet. Two hard-sided carriers were pictured in that scene. In a third scene, a blue hard-sided carrier with two cats inside almost fell off the hood of a car. In a fourth scene, two people showed up: one holding a cat that was in heat and another holding a grey hard-sided carrier by the handle.

My analysis: I'm glad cat carriers were used and pictured on this show. Considering the show's setting, it makes sense more expensive carriers like backpacks and rolling carriers weren't used.

SCHITT'S CREEK
Season 2 Episode 10
"Ronnie's Party" (2016)

One of the supporting characters in this Canadian sitcom was a vet named Dr. Theodore "Ted" Mullens. Multiple episodes had scenes in his vet clinic, but only one episode showed cat carriers. In this episode, a woman named Doris was sitting in the reception room, waiting for her cat, Mittens. She had a hard-sided cat carrier with screws. There was a shelving unit with three hard-sided cat carriers on the bottom shelf in the same room. Later in the episode, Alexis, one of the main characters on the show, broke the news to Doris that Mittens died.

My analysis: This was another missed opportunity to show different types of cat carriers. Only hard-sided carriers were shown.

FULLER HOUSE
Season 1 Episode 4 "The Not-So-Great Escape" (2016) and Season 3 Episode 12 "Fast Times at Bayview High" (2017)

The main character on this reboot of *Full House* was a vet named Dr. DJ Tanner-Fuller. Many scenes took place in her vet clinic. In "The Not-So-Great Escape" episode where a skunk was brought into the vet clinic, there were three grey hard-sided carriers under the metal table in the exam room. No soft-sided carriers or other types of carriers were shown. In the "Fast Times at Bayview High" episode where an alligator was brought into the clinic, Dr. Fuller's coworker, Dr. Matt Harmon, put a cat back into a grey top-loading hard-sided carrier.

My analysis: Maybe the props department only had hard-sided carriers. Only showing hard-sided cat carriers is better than not having any cat carriers at all in a vet clinic setting, but introducing various carrier types would make the show more realistic.

CARTOONS

CAT REBEL BY NATE FAKES

In this cartoon, a cat gets called a "hard-core" rebel by two other cats because he likes riding in a carrier and enjoys vet visits.

My analysis: As funny as this cartoon is, my goal with this book is to help more cats enjoy riding in cat carriers and going to the vet. The rebel in me is challenging the stereotype that all cats hate their cat carriers.

OFF THE MARK BY MARK PARISI

This award-winning newspaper cartoonist has drawn cat carriers in at least twelve cartoons. Here's a description of six cartoons that poke fun at how hard it is to get cats into cat carriers.

1) *Pet Vac*: A woman uses a vacuum cleaner to suck her cat into a hard-sided carrier, allowing her to get to the vet "fast and easy." (Please don't try this at home. For entertainment purposes only.)

2) *Scratching Cat Resists Pet Carrier Arrest*: A person with scratches, torn clothing, and disheveled hair is standing next to a hard-sided carrier with a cat inside. The cat is wondering if his sentence will be longer "for resisting arrest."

3) *Cat Carrier of Horror*: How humans see cat carriers is juxtaposed with how cats see carriers as monsters that want to eat them.

4) *Annoying Cat Games Keep Owner Young*: One of the ways cats keep you young is by making you play hide and seek when you're trying to get them into a cat carrier.

5) *Cat Owner Extreme Sports*: One of the "Xtreme sports for cat owners" is "the stuff and carry" because it can be so hard to get a cat into a carrier.

6) *Cat Alien Abduction*: One alien cat got mad at another alien cat for letting the man see the carrier because "now [they'll] never find him." This is a parody of scaredy-cats hiding when humans let them see their carrier. See page 53 for more info on scaredy-cats.

My analysis of these cartoons: Even though this cartoon series is called Off the Mark, the humour and observations about cat carriers are very much on the mark.

All the cat carriers in the Off the Mark cartoons are hard-sided carriers when there are so many other types of carriers now.

I drew many cartoons with carriers that aren't hard-sided!

SIMON'S CAT: OFF TO THE VET (2015)

In this episode of the web cartoon, Simon's cat got stung by a bee and needed to be seen by a vet. Simon had trouble getting his cat into a hard-sided carrier with only one door on the side. He used food as bait and a blanket to wrap his cat. He showed up at the vet clinic with an empty cat carrier, thinking his cat was in it, and had to make another trip. His cat acted like a gymnast (sticking his legs out to prevent going into the carrier), a fighter (growling, scratching, kicking, and throwing objects at Simon), and an opera singer (meowing loudly) on the way to the vet.

Waiting in the reception room of the vet clinic were the following: a dog on a leash, a guinea pig that a little girl took out of her pocket, and later a parrot outside of a cage. Simon's cat hit the dog and the guinea pig through the carrier door. The dog tried to catch the guinea pig.

Once Simon and his cat were in the exam room, he had trouble getting his cat out of the carrier. First, he tried to dump and shake his cat out of the carrier. Then he tried to pull his cat out of the carrier and got bitten.

My analysis: This cartoon is a comical depiction of what happens to many people and their cats. Cats can't throw objects at humans, thankfully, but

For info on different cat purrsonalities, see page 51.

people have shown up at the vet with empty carriers, thinking their cats were inside!

I could tell this wasn't Simon's first time struggling to get his cat into a carrier based on the way he was trying to trick his cat to get into the carrier. He should've put food inside the carrier instead of outside of the carrier. He should've also tried standing the carrier up with the open door facing the ceiling and putting his cat in back feet first.

Since Simon's cat was showing severe signs of stress and aggression, giving him a calming medication such as gabapentin before his vet appointment would've helped.

Lastly, again, I don't recommend taking cats, small mammals, or birds to the vet without carriers or cages. It might be comical to see animals chasing each other in a veterinary reception room in a cartoon but not in real life where animals can get seriously injured or killed.

OTHER

A fake ad was circulating online about a new feline transportation system called the Tabby Tote. On one end of the fake device is a screw, and on the other end is a muzzle. "A few extra turns of the stabilizer screw and your cat will be safely secured and unable to use your leg as a scratching post . . .

"Dr. Maimes Dobson of Focus on the Feline asserts that sometimes your kitty needs 'tough love,' and nothing on the market provides a more effective way to mold your special cat into the well-mannered creature . . ."

My analysis: I know there are people who found this fake ad meme funny, but it took things way too far. NO vet would recommend this highly unethical feline transportation system. I'm so glad it does NOT exist. Using it'd be a form of animal abuse or torture, not tough love. On top of that, this device wouldn't prevent other animals from attacking your cat or provide any crash protection during transportation.

BEFORE YOU USE A CAT CARRIER

It's time for you to leave for your cat's vet appointment. You pick up your cat to put it into the carrier. Your cat refuses to go in and runs under the bed to hide. With many scratches and dust bunnies, you later you arrive at the vet clinic late and stressed. Or maybe you have to cancel your appointment because you couldn't get your cat out from under the bed. What could've you done differently?

- Take your carrier out a few days before a vet appointment, not on the day of. Better yet, leave it out all the time with the door(s) open so your cat gets acclimated to it.

- Schedule extra time to get your cat into the carrier. This way, you won't be running late, you won't miss your appointment, and you won't have to rush, which can add extra stress.

- Check the traffic or public transportation schedule ahead of time.

- Clean your carrier before you use it, especially if you didn't clean it after you last used it. No cat wants to lie in a carrier with dust, cobwebs, poop, vomit, urine, etc. For cat urine, use an enzymatic cleaner. Water, baking soda, and vinegar can't remove the odour of urine. For infectious or contagious diarrhea, to prevent reinfecting your cat and infecting other cats, use diluted bleach at a ratio of 1:32 or 1 cup of bleach in a gallon of water (60 ml/litre). (For more info on what cleaners or disinfectants to use, see page 109.) Regardless of what cleaner you use, make sure the carrier is dry before you put your cat in it.

- Remove any non-cat items that you might have stored in the carrier. Your cat would be more comfortable if they didn't have to lie in a carrier with cleaning supplies, paintbrushes, etc.

- Check it for damage:

  Are there any loose, missing, or broken parts such as clips, pegs, screws, and zippers? The best time to find out about damage to your carrier is when there's no cat inside that can fall out or escape from it. Replace any missing or broken parts with equivalent parts if you can.

  If screws are missing from your hard-sided carrier, please don't use zip ties that are frowned upon by veterinary staff—they're difficult to remove if the lid of the carrier needs to be taken off to get your cat out gently. Zip ties can also break.

  If door pieces are missing or broken, please don't use sticks or chopsticks. They can break if a cat were to push on the door of the carrier, allowing your cat to escape.

  If carrier parts can't be replaced with equivalent parts, invest in a new carrier . . . sooner rather than later because you don't know when a medical emergency or a non-medical emergency such as a fire will require you to take your cat out of your house.

- Put a piece of clothing with your scent on it inside the carrier.

- Also, put a towel or blanket and a pee pad inside the carrier to make the carrier more comfortable and to absorb urine, vomit, or diarrhea from your cat.

- To help your cat feel more secure in the carrier, spray the carrier with a calming cat pheromone. Pheromones are species-specific hormone-like substances that affect the behaviour, emotions, and interactions of animals when they smell them. Use the spray fifteen minutes before putting your cat in the carrier to let the alcohol in the spray evaporate; otherwise, it can irritate your cat's airways. Don't spray the carrier with your cat inside. And don't spray it directly on your cat.

- If needed, give your cat a calming supplement prior to using a carrier for travel. For more info, see page 107.

- For more severe cases of stress, with your vet's go-ahead, give your cat a calming medication such as gabapentin a couple of hours before using a carrier.

- Label your cat carrier the way you'd label your luggage. You'd be surprised how many people have the same or similar-looking carrier that could get mixed up at the vet. If your carrier already has a label, make sure it's up to date. I've seen carriers labelled with the previous deceased cat's name, not the current cat's name.

For more info on pheromones, see page 107.

I WANT TO SEE YOU BE BRAVE.

Here are some benefits of having a carrier-trained cat:

1. Fewer injuries to the cat, cat owner, groomer, and/or veterinary staff

2. Reduced stress for the cat in the carrier

3. Reduced stress during car rides and vet exams (Pratsch et al., 64)

4. Reduced stress for the cat owner

5. Increased ability to take your cat to the vet or groomer (fewer no-show appointments)

Reward your cats with their favourite treat or food when they:

1. Approach the carrier

2. Step partway into the carrier

3. Step completely inside the carrier

4. Stay inside the carrier with the door open

5. Stay inside with the door closed

6. Are picked up in the carrier

7. Are carried around the room in the carrier

If your carrier comes apart, you can start with just the bottom of the carrier and later introduce the top of the carrier.

Carrier training a cat is like crate training a dog. Cats can be trained too, not just dogs.

A SAFE PLACE: MY CAT BOO LIKES TO NAP AND GROOM HIMSELF IN HIS BACKPACK CARRIER

Try to stay calm before and while putting your cat into a carrier. Cats are good at reading human body language and can feed off your fear, anxiety, and stress. Check out the cat carrier-themed meditation on page 85 to help you relax.

Practise using the cat carrier regularly. If you only use a carrier once a year, it's hard to be good at getting your cat into and out of it. Emergencies requiring the use of a carrier can happen unexpectedly. Please don't wait till there's an emergency to learn how to get your cat into and out of a carrier.

Leave your carrier out for your cat to sleep, play, and eat in. This way, your cat will get used to it and will be less scared of it. The carrier is a lot scarier if the only time your cat sees it is when it's time to see the vet.

A clicker can be used to carrier train a cat.

CARRIER TRAINING

For more info on carrier training, see page 107.

Tip: *Leaving your carrier out in your home is worthwhile for your cat's wellbeing.*

HOW TO GET YOUR CAT INTO A CARRIER

Set yourself up for success by following the tips in the previous section about things to do before using a cat carrier, like carrier training your cat and calming your own nerves. Where you choose to put your cat into a carrier also makes a difference, especially if you have a scaredy-cat. The bathroom is a good place to put your cat into a carrier, not the bedroom or living room. You want a small room:

1. Without furniture that your cat can hide under

2. With a door that can be closed so you don't have to chase your cat around the house

3. Without other pets and kids getting in the way

- Entice your cat into the carrier using high-value treats, wet food, a laser pointer, catnip, or silver vine.

- If your cat doesn't willingly go into the carrier, gently pick your cat up and hold the front/back legs together to prevent splaying when putting your cat into the carrier.

- If putting your cat in headfirst doesn't work, try putting your cat back end first. If your carrier only has one door on the side and your cat won't go in, turn your carrier so the door is facing the ceiling*. Then lower your cat in back end first and close the door before setting the carrier down.

*If the carrier falls over when it's on its side, put it up against the wall.

THINGS THAT HELP

MSY

If the previous techniques are not successful, another technique is to wrap your cat up in a towel or blanket. Then place the cat burrito or "purrito" into the carrier.

"PURRITO":
CAT-WRAPPING
TECHNIQUE

Wrapping a cat in a towel is also useful for other tasks such trimming the nails, cleaning the ears, and administering medication. It's possible to towel train cats: to get them to willingly lie down on a towel and be wrapped in exchange for a favourite treat.

For more tips on how to wrap a cat in a towel, see page 109.

MAGIC TOWEL: *TOWELS CAN HELP YOU DO MANY THINGS.*

- Some people find it easier to place the carrier off the ground, e.g., on a counter or a chair, when putting their cat into the carrier. Just make sure the carrier doesn't fall off with your cat inside.

- Try to remain calm during the process of putting your cat into a cat carrier. Yelling at your cat, cursing, etc., won't help your cat's fear, anxiety, or stress level.

- The best time to put cats into carriers is when they're sleepy or relaxed, not when they're already stressed.

AFTER YOU GET YOUR CAT INTO THE CARRIER:

- Make sure the carrier's door(s) or zippers are closed properly prior to departure.

- Reward your cat with praise and/or their favourite treat. Positive reinforcement, discipline with pleasant or desirable outcomes, works better than negative reinforcement or punishment.

- Pick your carrier up a short distance to see if the carrier holds. It wouldn't be good for your carrier to fall apart high up in the air with your cat inside.

- For scaredy-cats, cover the carrier with a towel or blanket sprayed with a calming cat pheromone.

WHEN YOU GET TO THE VET CLINIC WITH YOUR CAT IN A CARRIER

- Please don't open your cat carrier until you're safely inside an exam room with the door closed. Definitely don't open the carrier when you're on the curb outside the vet clinic because your cat could bolt and get lost or hit by a car. Don't even open the carrier in the reception room because your cat could escape and get attacked by a dog waiting in the reception room. Someone entering the clinic could also open the front door and inadvertently let your cat out.

- Put your carrier on your lap, on the seat next to you, or up on a counter or other surface off the ground instead of on the floor so people don't trip over your carrier and people's feet don't spook your cat (if your carrier isn't covered with a towel). Cats usually feel more secure when they're up high.

- Turn your carrier so your cat is facing you, not other cats or dogs, if your cat is cat-reactive or scared of dogs.

IF YOUR CAT DOESN'T WILLINGLY LEAVE THE CARRIER:

- ✗ Don't scruff (grip the loose skin at the back of a cat's neck) and pull your cat out.
- ✗ Don't dump your cat out.
- ✔ Entice your cat to leave the carrier with high reward treats or wet food.
- ✔ If your cat likes chasing laser pointers, bring one with you to entice your cat out of the carrier.
- ✔ Try a different door if your carrier has more than one door. Cats in carriers with a top-loading door can be gently lifted out of the top of the carrier.
- ✔ If your carrier has a lid that can be removed, take the lid off and then gently lift your cat out.

SCENARIO 1:

You made it to the vet clinic with your cat in a carrier, hopefully without any bites or scratches. Now, you're in the exam room, and your cat refuses to come out of the carrier. Given how much your cat dislikes the carrier, you thought they'd automatically come out on their own, but they won't. You've tried scruffing and pulling them out, but your cat is at the back of the carrier, hissing, growling, and swatting. The staff at the vet clinic have to use welding or animal-handling gloves to get your cat out of the carrier. What could've you done differently?

Please don't scruff and pull cats out of carriers. It's better to encourage them to leave the carrier on their own with something positive like treats or, if it's a hard-sided carrier, to take the lid off and then gently lift them out.

SCENARIO 2:

Your senior cat hasn't eaten in several days, so you have to make a trip to the vet. After you finally manage to get your cat into the carrier (somehow your cat still has the energy to fight you), you notice several of the screws on your carrier are missing, so you use zip ties in lieu of screws. The remaining screws are rusty. The handle of the door on your hard-sided carrier is also broken and doesn't close properly, so you zip tie it.

It's not just about getting cats into carriers and keeping cats inside the carriers. The cats have to be taken out to be examined, medicated, etc. The zip ties and rusty screws make it hard to get your cat out. Try to set your veterinary staff up for success so they can help your cats without getting bitten and scratched.

Veterinary staff, see the *Cat Carrier Tips for Vet Clinics* on page 100.

AFTER YOU USE A CAT CARRIER

There's a lot of info on how to get a cat into and out of a carrier, but what about after you use the carrier? Hardly anyone talks about what to do with the cat carrier after your trip to the vet, groomer, etc. A lot of people put the carrier away and forget about it until the next time they have to use it.

HERE ARE SOME TIPS FOR WHAT TO DO AFTER USING A CAT CARRIER:

- Check it for damage. See page 21 for more info.

- Clean it.

  This might seem like a no-brainer, but I've found dried vomit and urine in cat carriers from previous trips to the vet. Being dirty would displease most cats. Leaving urine in the carrier can also encourage cats to continue urinating in the carrier. Another reason to clean the carrier after each use is you might need it in an emergency situation where there's no time to clean. For more info on what cleaners or disinfectants to use at home, see pages 21 and 109.

- Leave your cat carrier out and feed your cat in it instead of putting it away right away when you get home.

  Associating the carrier with something positive will make the carrier less scary to your cat. If you have space, leave your carrier out all the time for your cat to sleep, play, and eat in it.

- If you don't have space to leave your carrier out all the time, store it somewhere that's:

  1. easily accessible in case of an emergency

  2. clean

  3. dry so metallic parts in your carrier (e.g., door handle, zippers, screws) don't rust

- Reward your cat with praise, attention, toys, and/or their favourite treat after using a carrier.

- Let your cat self-soothe after using a carrier. If that means sleeping with their favourite blanket on the couch, let them.

If you and your cat had a positive experience with the carrier, share it with your friends and family who have cats. They might not be aware of the type of carrier you have and might need tips and tricks to help them get their cat into and out of their carrier.

See answers below.

ANSWERS

1. The bottom carrier has a top-loading door.
2. The bottom has clips instead of screws.
3. The top carrier has a zip tie instead of clips.
4. The top carrier has a twist tie instead of clips.
5. The top carrier has a different type of door handle (spring-loaded) than the carrier on the right.
6. The top carrier has a chopstick in the door.
7. The top carrier has a crack in the side.
8. The handle of the top carrier is loose.
9. There's poop smeared on the inside of the top carrier.
10. One of the pawprint-shaped windows in the top carrier is missing a toe.

I DON'T HAVE TO HAVE THIS ALL SOLVED TODAY.

 THE INS AND OUTS OF CAT CARRIERS

Here are some short, real-life anecdotes not meant to scare people from using cat carriers but meant to be cautionary tales:

"Someone brought a cat in a carrier with an uncovered axe. The owner said she put the axe in the carrier when she was moving."

Please check your carrier before putting your cat in it. Also, sharp tools or weapons shouldn't be stored in cat carriers.

"An owner brought a cat in a pillowcase . . . [The cat] was terrified and gasping for breath."

"Cats that come in laundry baskets (with blanket bungee-corded over top) or pillowcases are the worst—so scary for the cats! Just trembling in there."

"No laundry baskets with oven racks tied on top!!"

Laundry baskets are for laundry, not for cats, as much as they like lying in them. Pillowcases are for pillows, not for cats.

"A cat arrived at the clinic with blood on his nose and a broken nail from trying to force his way out of his hard-sided carrier."

A calming medication such as gabapentin given a couple of hours before placing the cat in the carrier could've prevented the self-trauma. Carrier training would've helped too.

"A cat had its nail ripped off as it panicked and got it stuck in one of the holes [in a hard-sided carrier]. They had to amputate the toe."

Cat owners should invest time to try to make the carrier less stressful (training, positive reinforcement, etc.).

"A cat was in a [hard-sided] carrier with only one door, and the lid was securely screwed in. We stressed the cat out so much trying to reach in and pull the cat out that it eventually attacked one of my coworkers by jumping on top of his head and then quickly hiding back [in] the carrier."

It's a lot easier and less stressful getting cats out of carriers with snap on/snap off lids and with more than one door.

"[Carrier] door zip tied shut, half carrier screwed, and half carrier zip tied closed, cat upset, two zip ties broke on the side when carrier lifted onto exam table and cat attempted escape through side and got stuck, becoming even more upset . . ."

Please don't use zip ties on cat carriers.

"Someone's young kid put one arm and her head into the carrier. She got stuck while the cat inside was hissing and swatting at her!"

Kids can be over-affectionate and may want to help, not realizing they can get hurt by their cat.

"Once I was doing an exam at a high-volume/low income SPCA clinic. The client brought the cat in a dirty carrier. As I took the lid off to get the kitty out, to my horror, a ton of tiny little cockroaches skittered out from under the rim, and began to crawl over the exam table and up the walls . . ."

I probably would've screamed and run out of the exam room if this happened during one of my appointments. I know other vets who'd do the same if spiders crawled out of a carrier.

CAT CARRIER HORROR STORIES

"I found a ton of flea dirt in a cat carrier. Raccoons and feral cats sleep in the carrier that the owner leaves outside."

Please store your cat carrier inside to prevent your pets from getting fleas and other infectious diseases from wildlife and feral cats and to prevent your carrier from getting rusty. (If you want to help feral cats, you can buy outdoor cat houses or make feral cat shelters out of totes or coolers.)

"Cardboard carrier: cats literally eating their way out of them. (All the time! Especially with kittens.)"

Cardboard carriers aren't recommended for cats that like chewing cardboard.

". . . A client flew a kitten over from Toronto and lost him on the airplane as he did not fully close the carrier."

Always make sure the carrier is closed (during travel). There are a lot of places for a kitten to hide on a plane.

A cat escaped from its carrier "when it was in transit from the cargo warehouse to the plane . . . The cat [might have been] roaming somewhere in the airport field and . . . it might [have been] caught by one of the airport's hawks or eagles that keep runways clear for planes." (Devlin, 2022)

To prevent your cat from escaping on the plane or at the airport, check your cat carrier to make sure none of the components are broken or loose prior to travel and make sure the carrier is closed.

" . . . A big cat [fell through] the bottom of a cardboard carrier."

Cardboard carriers aren't recommended for heavy cats. If you have to use one for a big cat, hold it like a present with both hands under it, not by the handle.

For more horror stories of cats escaping at the airport, see page 108.

"The handle of a hard-sided carrier broke off, and the cat slammed to the floor."

Hold a hard-sided carrier like a present with both hands under it, not by the handle, especially if your cat is heavy.

"Someone brought both of her adult cats in the same carrier. Even though they're littermates that normally get along, when they were waiting in the reception area, they started fighting. They were in such a bad mood that it was hard for the vet to examine them."

Even if your cat carrier is big enough for two adult cats, please use separate carriers or dual-compartment carriers. For more info, see pages 37 and 93.

"This week a lady was a half hour late to her appointment because she brought her cat to the clinic with no carrier, just free in her car, and it got stuck under the seat. She couldn't get the cat out, and my receptionist had to go out and extricate the cat from the bowels of her car."

Please, please—if you don't have a carrier, get one or ask to borrow one (from your vet clinic)! You can pick it up in advance, bring your cat in it, take them home, and then return it the next day. They're happy to loan it to you short term.

"A cat was in a [soft-sided] carrier in the car, which was not secured. [The] owner took a sharp turn and some other belongings from the car fell onto the carrier (and kitty)."

Use a seat belt to secure your cat carrier. Avoid sharp turns while driving. Stow away items that can fall onto the carrier during a drive.

"A fractious cat got the long nails on one paw stuck in the mesh of a soft-sided carrier that didn't hold its shape. The owner and I tried to unstick her nails and to zip up the carrier as she was swiping at us with the other paw, but we weren't able to. We ended up having to put the soft-sided carrier with the cat inside into the clinic's loaner hard-sided carrier so she could be safely transported home."

For cats that swipe at people through the mesh and/or get nails caught in mesh, invest in a hard-sided carrier with a lid on top.

"A cat in a carrier hit the windshield when the owner had to suddenly brake to avoid hitting a car that pulled in front of them."

Securely fasten a carrier in place by clipping it in with a seat belt.

Many veterinary staff shared horror stories of cats escaping in the parking lot outside vet clinics. Here are the worst ones:

"A carrier fell apart in the parking lot of a strip mall because the rusty screws broke. The cat escaped . . ."

If the screws in your carrier are rusty, the carrier needs to be replaced.

"When I was a new grad, I helped a client put her cat into her carrier. It was a hard-sided carrier with a door handle on a spring that needs to be pulled up. The door wasn't latched properly, and the cat escaped in the parking lot on the way to the car. I don't know if the cat was ever found."

If you use a hard-sided carrier, make sure the door is latched properly before stepping outside.

"A cat pushed his head through the dual zippers in his soft-sided carrier and escaped in the parking lot."

If you use a soft-sided carrier with dual zippers, move the two sliders to the side where your cat can't reach them or use a paper clip to connect the two pull tabs, AKA pullers. There are carriers with zippers that have safety clips; i.e., the zipper pull tabs clip together so cats can't push the zippers open.

"I had to chase a cat not in a carrier that a client brought in his arms and a dog spooked it [in the parking lot]."

The dog could've attacked the cat. The cat could've been hit by a car. The cat could've gotten lost.

"Once had a cat escape a carrier in the parking lot and ended up climbing into the underside of the owner's car. The cat then proceeded to attack her when she tried to get it out, resulting in an ER visit."

This horror story highlights how it's not just unsafe for cats to escape in parking lots but also unsafe for cat owners.

The worst cat carrier horror story I've heard:

"During COVID, when we were doing curbside pickup, a cat kept crying in his carrier outside the clinic. The client opened the carrier, hoping to console his cat. Unfortunately, the cat fled, ran across a busy street, got hit by a vehicle, and died."

Poor kitty, rest in peace.

Please don't open a cat carrier outside near a busy street when your cat is scared.

TOMORROW IS A BRAND-NEW DAY.

It's not all doom and gloom. Here are some happier cat carrier stories where no cats escaped and no cats or humans were injured:

"One of [the] cats went into the carrier to keep the other one company when she did not even have to!"

It's definitely possible for cats to willingly go into a carrier, whether it's to support another cat or to go on an adventure.

"It used to be that every time I had to take my cat to the vet, I was stressed out for days before the appointment, just thinking about the struggle of getting her into the carrier. Then I figured out the solution: I get my husband to put the cat into the carrier. My cat loves my husband and will do anything for him including going into a carrier."

Sometimes it's better to get another person who's calmer and who has a stronger bond with the cat to put them into the carrier.

"Using a laser light to get the cat inside. Works once so be ready to shut the door without fail!"

This method doesn't work for every cat, but if it does, great! Less stress and less force needed to get a cat into a carrier.

"I've had success stories with removable top carriers with cats that were previously lunging from other styles."

Carriers with removable tops or lids are the #1 preferred cat carriers by veterinary staff. For more info, see page 14.

"The type of carrier with a bottom that pulls out like a drawer makes it so much easier to take a cat out of a carrier!"

Just make sure the cat doesn't jump all the way to the back and get squished by the drawer when putting the cat back into the carrier.

CELEBRATE SUCCESS.

FREQUENTLY ASKED QUESTIONS

Many websites have FAQs. I wanted to include them in this book too. To be honest, this section should be called Questions I Wish People Asked Their Vet about Cat Carriers. These questions aren't asked frequently, or at all, when they should be.

QUESTION #1:

Why do vets recommend cat carriers?

Carriers are essential for the safety of cats while being transported. Other cats and dogs in the reception room of the vet clinic can attack or spook your cat. Your cat can jump out of your arms, run away, get lost, or worse, get hit by a car. If you're driving with your cat loose, your cat can go under your brake pedal, distract you from your driving, and cause a collision. If a collision occurs, your cat can hit the windshield, get crushed, etc.

QUESTION #2:

What if my cat doesn't like the carrier?

Your cat's safety comes first. Here's an analogy: What if your kid doesn't like wearing a bike helmet or a seat belt? They still need to wear them. Just as not using a helmet or seat belt puts your kid at risk, not using a carrier puts your cat at risk.

You can try a different type of carrier. Some cats prefer one type over another. You can also carrier train your cat to help your cat adjust to the carrier better. See the carrier training tips outlined on page 23. A 2018 study showed carrier training cats reduces stress during car rides and vet exams (Pratsch et al., 64).

QUESTION #3:

How big a carrier should I get? Is it one size fits all? Is it the bigger the better?

Carriers aren't one size fits all. The size of carrier to get depends on the size of your cat. Some carriers specify the size or weight of cat recommended to fit in the carrier. If the carrier doesn't have specifications, a good rule of thumb is one and half times the size of your cat. Measure the length of your cat from the tip of the nose to the base of the tail and the height from the tip of the ears to the bottom of the paws. Multiply the length and height by 1.5 and compare it to the length and height of the carrier.

Another rule of thumb is to choose a carrier that's big enough for your cat to stand up, to turn around in, and to lie down without feeling cramped. Cats are more likely to be stressed and aggressive when they feel cramped.

In the opposite scenario, when a carrier is too big for a cat, the cat can slide from one end to the other, causing fear, stress, and anxiety. A bigger carrier also makes it easier for cats to evade you when you're taking them out by going to the back or to the other end of the carrier. Plus, the bigger the carrier, the harder it is to carry. Don't buy a carrier that's much bigger than your cat.

The exception to this rule is when you have a kitten. Buy a carrier that'll fit the anticipated full-grown size unless you plan to buy another, bigger carrier later.

QUESTION #4:

How can I prevent getting bitten and scratched when getting my cat into and out of a carrier?

Use a towel or blanket to wrap your cat. Wear long sleeves. Trim your cat's nails before using the carrier. Positive reinforcement, carrier training, calming pheromones, and pre-visit pharmaceuticals, such as gabapentin, will help reduce fear associated with the carrier, thereby preventing fear-based aggression.

QUESTION #5:

Where should I put my cat carrier?

At home: If you have the space, leave your cat carrier out as a safe place for your cat. If you do have to put away your cat carrier, store it in an easily accessible place in case of emergencies and disasters that require immediate evacuation.

At the vet clinic: Put cat carriers up high on a table or counter. Just make sure the carrier isn't going to fall over the edge of the counter if the cat moves. It's not recommended to put carriers on the ground, where cats can feel insecure. Another reason to avoid leaving carriers on the ground is the risk of people tripping over them and potentially injuring themselves or the cat.

QUESTION #6:

Is putting two cats into one carrier recommended?

No. Unless you have two kittens or a mother and her kitten, please use two separate cat carriers. Most carriers don't have enough room for two adult cats. Being confined in a small carrier can trigger aggression between the two cats. (See the Horror Stories section on page 31 for more info.) Plus, having two adult cats in the same carrier makes it heavier and harder to carry.

There are special carriers with two compartments, one for each cat. For examples of dual-compartment carriers, see page 93.

QUESTION #7:

If I have more than one cat, how many carriers should I have?

Ideally one carrier per cat in case there's an emergency or disaster that requires evacuation of all of your cats. If cost is a concern, check your local thrift store or Buy Nothing group for cat carriers. If space is a concern, there are a variety of collapsible cat carriers that fold flat. See the section on collapsible cat carriers on page 44 as well as the unsponsored list of collapsible cat carriers on page 96.

There are people who have more than one carrier per cat. Why? For different purposes: one for adventures outside and one for going to the vet. If you have the budget for more than one carrier, that's great, but it's by no means a necessity. I'd be happy if you had one good carrier instead of two cheap carriers or no carrier at all.

QUESTION #8:

Where can I get a cat carrier from?

- **Online:** Most cat carriers are available for sale online. In the Additional Resources section on page 93, there's a non-exhaustive, unsponsored list of different types of carriers with websites, if available.

- **Pet stores:** The selection of carriers in pet stores isn't as extensive as it is online, but in today's global economy, one can find products in-store from all over the world. I once found a uniquely designed cat carrier from Italy in a pet store in Canada.

- **Vet clinics:** The most common type of cat carrier available at vet clinics is the cardboard carrier.

- **Department stores**
- **Home furnishing stores**
- **Thrift stores**
- **Buy Nothing group**

Take the *Should You Get A New Cat Carrier* quiz on page 58.

QUESTION #9:

When is it time to replace my carrier?

It's time to invest in a new cat carrier if:

1. **Your old carrier is broken and/or rusty.** This can jeopardize your cat's safety. Your cat's safety is the number 1 priority.

2. **Your cat doesn't fit in the old carrier.** See page 36 for more info.

3. **Your cat carrier doesn't meet your physical needs.** E.g., a cat backpack is great for hikers but not for those who have an injured shoulder.

4. **Your cat prefers a different type of carrier.** Cats have preferences too.

5. **Your cat carrier is badly soiled and can't be cleaned properly.** Some types of carriers are difficult to clean and can't be thrown into the washing machine to wash out urine, vomit, diarrhea, blood, etc.

6. **Your carrier brings back sad or bad memories of your previous cat.** It's best to associate the cat carrier with positive experiences.

QUESTION #10:

How do I choose what type of carrier to get? There are so many different types of carriers.

It isn't one type or one size fits all. Unless it's an emergency, I don't recommend just walking into a pet store and buying any carrier off the shelf. More carriers are available online. To prevent buyer's remorse, before buying a carrier, do research, look up reviews, ask your vet, and keep reading this book!

The type of carrier recommended for you/your cat depends on a variety of factors:

1. **Your cat's size**

   Cardboard carriers aren't recommended for heavy or large cats, but they'd be fine for kittens. Heavy or large cats are also harder to carry around in a backpack. A rolling carrier or stroller might be a better option.

2. **Your cat's personality**

   Some cats are shy and are happy to never leave their home. Others are curious and want to see the world. A curious outdoorsy cat would appreciate a backpack with a big window while a scaredy-cat wouldn't.

3. **Your needs and lifestyle**

   Do you have an active lifestyle? Will you be taking your cat hiking, camping, etc.? Do you have any physical limitations? If you have chronic shoulder or back pain, cat backpacks aren't the best type of carrier for you. Instead, consider a rolling carrier or pet stroller.

4. **Your budget**

   Most cat carriers are in the $50-$150 range, but less and more expensive options are available. Less expensive options include second-hand carriers from thrift stores. For free cat carriers, check your local Buy Nothing group. See the unsponsored list of cat carriers on page 93.

Here are some other factors to consider:

- **The weight of the carrier**

  If your cat is already heavy to begin with, avoid a cat carrier that has a heavy frame.

- **Number of doors or openings** (BONUS if there's a top-loading door or opening)

  The more doors or openings your carrier has, the greater the chance of getting your cat into or out of the carrier.

- **How easily the doors can be opened and closed**

  Some hard-sided cat carriers have doors that are difficult to line up and close. Some have spring-loaded door handles that aren't the easiest for people with arthritis in their hands.

- **How easily the carrier can be taken apart or how easily the lid can be taken off if it's a hard-sided carrier**

  Carriers that require tools such as screwdrivers to take apart and put back together aren't ideal. Screws are difficult to remove, easy to lose, and noisy when dropped, spooking cats. They can also get rusty, making them even more difficult to remove. Instead, look for cat carriers with easy clips or secure zippers.

- **Airline approval**

  Will your cat be flying with you? See the Air Travel with Your Cat section on page 61 for more info.

- **Crash test certification**

  Did you know there are carriers tested and proven to protect pets during a car crash? Will your cat be going on long car rides with you? For more info, see page 63.

- **Functionality of the carrier**

  If you like things to be multifunctional, there are cat carriers that also function as cat beds, cat tunnels, car seats, tents, and laptop/tablet sleeves. See the unsponsored list of cat carriers on page 93.

- **Reviews**

  See what others who've used the carrier say. People who've used the carrier might know about flaws in the carrier design even the manufacturer doesn't know about, e.g., the carrier's door handle breaks easily or the carrier has poor-fitting screws.

Take the *What Type of Carrier Best Suits You and Your Cat* quiz on page 59.

THE HISTORY OF CAT CARRIERS

Although human beings have had cats as pets for millennia, cats weren't always transported the way they are nowadays. Back in the day, vets were more likely to travel to people's homes to take care of animals than people were likely to transport their cats to the vet.

There's little information available on cat carriers used before the modern era. In the 1920s, there were carriers made of wicker. In the 1930s-1960s, the Alco brand made metal and leather carriers. Other antique or vintage carriers were made of wood. Eventually, hard plastic replaced wood and metal.

The shape of carriers also changed from looking like letter boxes or toolboxes with locks to rectangular prisms with one front-facing door and screws to secure the lid. Carriers from the 1920s-1960s are now rare, but carriers from the 1980s and 1990s (older than most support staff working in vet clinics) are still being used despite the screws being rusty and the availability of other types of carriers better designed for getting cats in and out.

In the late 1980s, Gayle Martz, a former TWA flight attendant, and photographer who worked in the handbag and fashion industry, invented the first airline-approved soft-sided pet carrier. She named it after her dog, Sherpa. By 1994, the Sherpa Bag had been approved by most airlines, thanks to her advocating for pet travel. See pages 108 and 111 for more info.

See page 111 for more info on vintage & antique cat carriers.

TYPES OF CAT CARRIERS

THINK OUTSIDE THE BOX

It used to be every cat owner got a hard-sided handheld carrier with only one door for their cat. Nowadays, there are many other types of carriers to choose from. Carriers can be categorized in different ways: handheld vs. hands-free, wheeled vs. non-wheeled, or portable bags vs. boxes vs. luggage. I categorized cat carriers by overall design.

Here are six types or categories of cat carriers:

- Hard-sided (handheld, no wheels)
- Soft-sided (handheld, no wheels)
- Backpacks (hands-free, no wheels, can be hard- or soft-sided)
- Collapsible carriers (handheld, no wheels, can be hard- or soft-sided)
- Cardboard carriers (technically, a type of collapsible carrier) (handheld, box, no wheels)
- Rolling carriers (with wheels like luggage, not hands-free, can be hard- or soft-sided)

Carriers can belong to more than one category. For example, there are carriers that are collapsible, soft-sided, and rolling at the same time. Keep reading to learn more about the six different types of cat carriers and their pros and cons!

HARD-SIDED CARRIERS

This type of carrier is one of the most common types, if not the most common type (page 47). It's also the most common type of carrier portrayed in popular media (page 16). The older or simpler hard-sided carriers have screws or pegs securing the lid and only one front-facing door. The newer or better designed hard-sided carriers have an additional top-loading door and/or a clip-on/clip-off lid that can be easily removed to get cats into and out of the carrier.

TIPS

- The trick for putting this type of carrier back together is to make sure the door lines up. If the front door isn't properly lined up, you won't be able to close the carrier. Make sure all the doors and latches are closed properly before departure.

- Pick a carrier with a top-loading door, not just one on the side. This feature makes it easier to get your cat into and out of the carrier.

- If your hard-sided carrier only has one door on the side and your cat won't go in, turn your carrier so the door is facing the ceiling. Then lower your cat in back end first and close the door before setting the carrier down.

- Line the bottom of the carrier with a towel for comfort and a pee pad for soaking up urine, vomit, or diarrhea.

- Although this type of carrier usually has a handle, when your cat is inside, hold the carrier like a present with both hands under it, not by the handle. This way of holding prevents swaying of the carrier, which can scare cats. Also, if the handle breaks, your carrier won't fall to the ground with your cat inside.

THIS HARD-SIDED CARRIER ISN'T IDEAL BECAUSE IT HAS SCREWS AND ONLY ONE FRONT-FACING DOOR.

PREVENT THE DOOR AND SCREWS FROM FALLING TO THE FLOOR AS THE LOUD NOISE OFTEN STARTLES CATS.

A DISASSEMBLED HARD-SIDED CARRIER WITH SCREWS

PROS

- ✔ Easiest to find at pet stores.
- ✔ Waterproof and easier to clean than other types of carriers.
- ✔ Newer designs have a bottom that slides out like a drawer, making it easier to get your cat out.
- ✔ Can be taken apart.
- ✔ Sturdy.

CONS

- ✘ Can be heavy.
- ✘ Can be tricky to put together.
- ✘ Some airlines only allow soft-sided carriers in the cabin.

Pro tip: *When reassembling a hard-sided carrier, first line up the side of the door that doesn't have a latch. (If both sides have a latch, pick one side to line up.) Once the carrier is assembled, close the door. This technique is easier than trying to line up both sides of the door simultaneously.*

SOFT-SIDED CARRIERS

One of the most common types of cat carriers—the soft-sided carrier—is made of fabric. In soft-sided carriers, zippers are used for closure instead of clips, pegs, or screws used in hard-sided carriers. I included purse carriers in this category of cat carriers.

TIPS

PUTTING YOUR CAT IN BACK END FIRST USUALLY WORKS BETTER THAN HEAD FIRST.

- Line the bottom of the carrier with a towel for comfort and a pee pad for soaking up urine, vomit, or diarrhea.

- Although this type of carrier usually has a handle, when your cat is inside, hold it like a present with both hands underneath. This prevents swaying of the carrier, which can scare cats. Also, if the handle breaks, your carrier won't fall to the ground with your cat inside.

- Get a soft-sided carrier with more than one door, especially one on top.

- How to put a cat into a soft-sided carrier that only has one front-facing opening: try standing the carrier up with the opening facing the ceiling. Put your cat into the carrier back end first.

TAPING THE TOWEL AND PEE PAD DOWN CAN PREVENT THEM FROM FALLING AWAY WHEN THE CARRIER IS TIPPED ON ITS SIDE.

PROS

✓ Easy to find in pet stores.

✓ No clips, pegs, or screws.

✓ Some are expandable.

✓ Certain designs are certified by the Center for Pet Safety (CPS). For more info, see pages 63, 93, and 108.

✓ Certain designs have wheels (either attached or detachable), adding versatility or portability.

CONS

✗ Smart cats can get the zipper open to escape, so get one with lockable zippers.

✗ Some designs cave in when the zipper or door is opened.

✗ Some designs have mesh that can trap your cat's nails.

✗ Some designs have pads on the bottom that cats can get underneath.

✗ Can't be taken apart to get fractious cats out.

✗ Most soft-sided carriers aren't waterproof.

✗ Usually harder to clean than hard-sided carriers.

THIS PARTICULAR SOFT-SIDED CARRIER ISN'T IDEAL BECAUSE IT ONLY HAS ONE OPENING.

BACKPACK CARRIERS

A newer invention, this type of cat carrier hasn't been around for as long as the hard-sided or soft-sided carrier. The backpack allows the cat to see the outside world through a window made of mesh or clear plastic. It can look like a space capsule or bubble.

I recommend backpacks that are fully enclosed. I don't recommend backpacks that have holes for the head plus or minus the legs. The exposed body parts are at risk of getting bitten or crushed.

PROS

- ✓ Portable: can be carried hands- free on one's back.
- ✓ Certain designs are expandable, providing more space for cats.
- ✓ Certain designs have a built-in laptop/tablet sleeve or a pocket for extra storage.
- ✓ Certain designs have a light and a fan to keep cats cool during travel.
- ✓ Great for curious cats that want to see the outside world.

CONS

- ✗ Transparent backpacks aren't recommended for scaredy-cats.
- ✗ Some cats get motion sickness in backpacks with a plastic bubble.
- ✗ In the summer, backpacks with a plastic bubble can overheat.
- ✗ Can be hard on your back and shoulders if your cat is heavy.
- ✗ Big cats might not have enough room to lie down.
- ✗ Attracts attention (expect comments, questions, and pictures taken by random strangers).
- ✗ Harder to clean; not all are machine-washable.

TIPS

- ☺ Choose a design with more than one opening to make it easier to get your cat in and out.
- ☺ Line the bottom of the carrier with a towel for comfort and a pee pad for soaking up urine, vomit, or diarrhea.

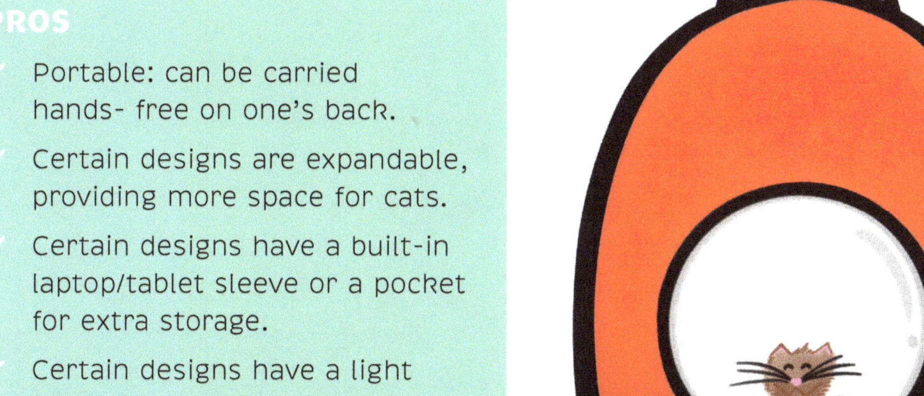

THE BUBBLE-STYLE OF BACKPACK CARRIER

ANOTHER STYLE OF BACKPACK CARRIER (FEATURING MY CAT BOO)

COLLAPSIBLE CARRIERS

This type of cat carrier isn't as common as hard-sided or soft-sided carriers. Some are made of hard plastic. Others are made of lightweight fabric (similar to what umbrellas are made of) with zippers. The distinguishing feature of this type of carrier is the ability to be folded flat for storage. It can be triangular, prism-shaped, or rectangular.

TIPS

- Although this type of carrier usually has a handle, when your cat is inside, hold the carrier like a gift with both hands under it. This way of holding prevents swaying of the carrier, which can scare cats. Also, if the handle breaks, your carrier won't fall to the ground with your cat inside.

- Line the bottom of the carrier with a towel for comfort and a pee pad for soaking up urine, vomit, or diarrhea.

PROS

- ✔ Good for storage, space-saving.
- ✔ Certain designs are certified by the Center for Pet Safety (CPS). For more info, see pages 63, 93, and 108.
- ✔ Certain designs are multi-functional (carrier, bed, tunnel, car seat, litter box +/- tent).
- ✔ Certain designs are light.

CONS

- ✗ Some only have one door.
- ✗ Hard to find in pet stores; order online.

CARDBOARD CARRIERS

I don't mean any cardboard box that appliances, cookware sets, or groceries come in—I mean a professionally designed box for cats with breathing holes, a top that closes, and a handle. Many newly adopted cats are sent home in this type of carrier (unless people donate more expensive carriers like the ones listed earlier in this book).

Cats can chew holes and dig their claws in the cardboard. There are videos online of cats chewing their way out of cardboard carriers and pushing their head through holes in cardboard carriers. The handle can also break, especially if your cat is heavy! The bottom can fall out too.

For these reasons, this type of carrier is usually just for temporary use. Transition your cat to a sturdier, more durable type of carrier. That said, it's better to have this type of carrier for transporting a cat than no carrier at all.

PROS

- ✓ Inexpensive, the least expensive of all the carriers.
- ✓ Recyclable.
- ✓ Light.
- ✓ Collapsible.
- ✓ Newer designs can also be used as perches or cat houses.
- ✓ Cats ♥ boxes.

CONS

- ✗ Not waterproof.
- ✗ Only one opening.
- ✗ Not sturdy or durable.

TIPS

- Make sure the cardboard carrier is assembled properly so the carrier doesn't break open on the bottom and so the top of the carrier can be closed properly.

- In case the handle tears or the bottom gives out, hold the carrier like a present with both hands under it, not by the handle.

- Line the bottom of the carrier with a towel for comfort and a pee pad for soaking up urine, vomit, or diarrhea.

- If there's an emergency requiring you to transport your cat and your regular carrier breaks, you can use a cardboard box with:

  - a lid or closed top to prevent escape

  - breathing holes for air circulation

  - a fully taped bottom to prevent injury and escape

  - no slits through which the cat can scratch people

  - a towel for comfort and/or accidents

  - a pee pad for accidents

ROLLING CARRIERS

This type of cat carrier is uncommon yet practical, especially for people with back or shoulder issues and for heavy cats. The distinguishing features of this type of carrier are the wheels and handle that allow you to pull your cat around like carry-on luggage.

TIPS

- Avoid rolling the carrier on bumpy surfaces that can stress your cat.
- Use wheelchair ramps.
- Certain soft-sided carriers can be converted into rolling carriers with a spinner wheelbase (page 97).
- I've seen people turn their hard-sided or soft-sided carriers into rolling carriers by strapping them to a dolly. Ensure the straps are securely fastened to prevent your carrier from falling off the dolly.
- Line the bottom of the carrier with a towel for comfort and a pee pad for soaking up urine, vomit, or diarrhea.

PROS

- ✔ Portable.
- ✔ Easy on the back and shoulders, so they're recommended for seniors and those with injuries.
- ✔ Some cats prefer the rolling movement over the swinging movement of other types of carriers.

CONS

- ✘ Hard to find in pet stores; order online.
- ✘ Some only have one door for the cat to go in or out.
- ✘ Not stair-friendly, need a ramp or elevator.
- ✘ Close to the ground when most cats feel safer up high.

MOST COMMON CARRIERS

Which type of cat carrier is the most common? The least common? Since I couldn't find any statistics, I kept a tally of the different types of cat carriers people brought to my appointments (including surgeries) for six months from January 1 to June 30, 2022, at seven different Canadian vet clinics where I was a locum or relief vet. These appointments were booked by receptionists, not by me, with cats of random ages and breeds.

Most cat carriers brought to my appointments were hard-sided. Most carriers shown on TV, in movies, and in cartoons were hard-sided as well. See page 16 for more info.

Next most popular were the soft-sided carriers, followed by backpack carriers. The rolling carrier was the least popular: 0%. That's why it's not even shown in this pie chart shaped like a cat track toy.

Others included: a pet hair-drying enclosure from overseas (fully enclosed except for the hole where a hair dryer would be inserted to dry a cat or dog—my first time seeing one in North America), a wire cage, and a dog crate. There was also a small percentage of cats not brought to the vet in a carrier or anything enclosed.

These were just my observations. Other vets might see more cats not in carriers and more of other types of cat carriers. The popularity of different types of cat carriers is influenced by:

- What local pet stores sell.
- The lifestyle of cat owners; e.g., outdoorsy people are more likely to have backpack carriers.
- Income level; e.g., lower-income people are probably not able to afford carriers >$200.
- Age group; e.g., older cat owners are more likely to still be using cat carriers from the 1980s or '90s. These were built to last but not necessarily built for ease of getting cats in or out.
- Social media trends—cat owners, especially younger ones, see ads and pictures of cat carriers online.

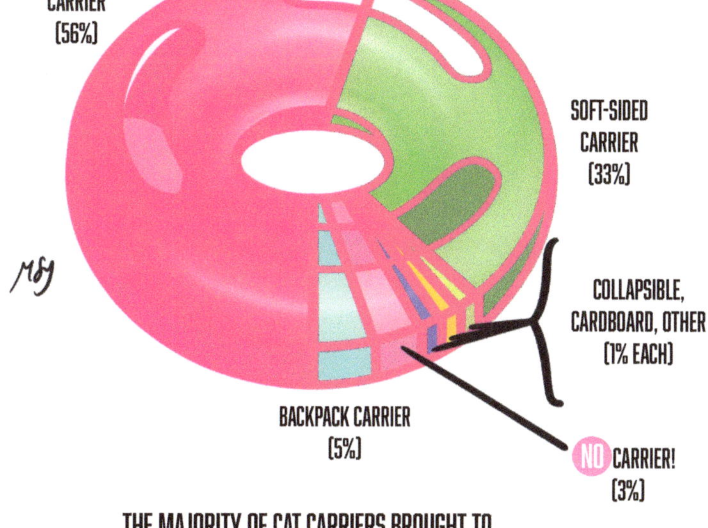

THE MAJORITY OF CAT CARRIERS BROUGHT TO MY APPOINTMENTS WERE HARD-SIDED.

A NOTE ON PET STROLLERS

Pet strollers aren't technically carriers, but they function like rolling carriers. Inspired by baby strollers, pet strollers are becoming increasingly common as more and more people are treating their cats like babies and as more people are giving their cats supervised outdoor time instead of letting them roam free or be couch potatoes.

TIPS

- If you let the cover of the stroller down, make sure your cat is securely fastened to prevent escape. Use caution around dogs that can attack your cat.

- Use wheelchair ramps and avoid rolling the carrier on bumpy surfaces that can stress your cat out.

- Line the bottom of the carrier with a towel for comfort and a pee pad for soaking up urine, vomit, or diarrhea.

PROS

- ✔ Raised off the ground. (Most cats feel safer up high.)

- ✔ Easier on the back and shoulders than most types of cat carriers, so they're recommended for seniors and those with injuries.

- ✔ Beneficial for joggers.

- ✔ Beneficial for pets who like sightseeing and fresh air.

- ✔ Extra items can be transported in the undercarriage of some models of pet strollers.

- ✔ Some models of pet strollers are designed for two pets.

- ✔ Some models of pet strollers can be folded up for storage.

- ✔ There are multi-functional strollers that serve as rolling carriers, regular carriers, backpacks, and more.

CONS

- ✖ People can judge you for treating your cat like a baby.

- ✖ Not stair-friendly, need a ramp or elevator.

- ✖ Expensive.

- ✖ Hard to find in pet stores; order online.

A NOTE ON PET SLINGS

AKA Sling Carriers or Pet Björns

Inspired by a baby product, the pet sling is a cloth product that goes over at least one shoulder and has a pocket for a pet. I didn't include the pet sling in the list of different types of carriers because it isn't completely enclosed. Your pet's head is usually exposed in a sling. Sometimes so are the legs. Pet slings don't provide protection from attacks or bites by other animals. I'd be even more wary if the sling doesn't have a clip to fasten your pet.

Horror story: "A kitten got spooked by dogs on a hike and jumped out of his sling. He was missing for an entire week up in the snowy mountains in the middle of winter!"

If you want to take your cat on hikes, make sure your cat is securely fastened in a cat carrier and/or on a leash to prevent mishaps like this.

Some people like using the pet sling because it's hands-free. I recommend using a fully enclosed cat backpack instead. It'll provide your cat with more security and protection than a sling.

A NOTE ON LEASHES AND HARNESSES

Leashes and harnesses are no longer only for dogs. Leashes prevent your cat from escaping when outside and allow control and leading of your cat. Attach the leash to a harness, not to your cat's collar, especially if it's a snap-off collar.

It used to be if you wanted to put a harness on a cat, you had to use a dog harness. Now, there are cat-specific harnesses designed to prevent contortionist cats from slipping out.

EXTRA FAQ:

Can I take my cat to the vet on a leash and harness without a carrier?

Having a leash and harness on your cat is better than nothing at all, but a cat carrier offers protection from other animals at the vet as well as crash protection in the car. Also, the carrier provides a safe (and hopefully familiar) place for your cat to hide and rest in while waiting at the vet clinic.

For more FAQs, see pages 36-39.

See page 93 for an unsponsored list of cat carriers, strollers, leashes, and harnesses.

WHO SAYS IT HAS TO BE HARD & UNCOMFORTABLE?

    THE INS AND OUTS OF CAT CARRIERS

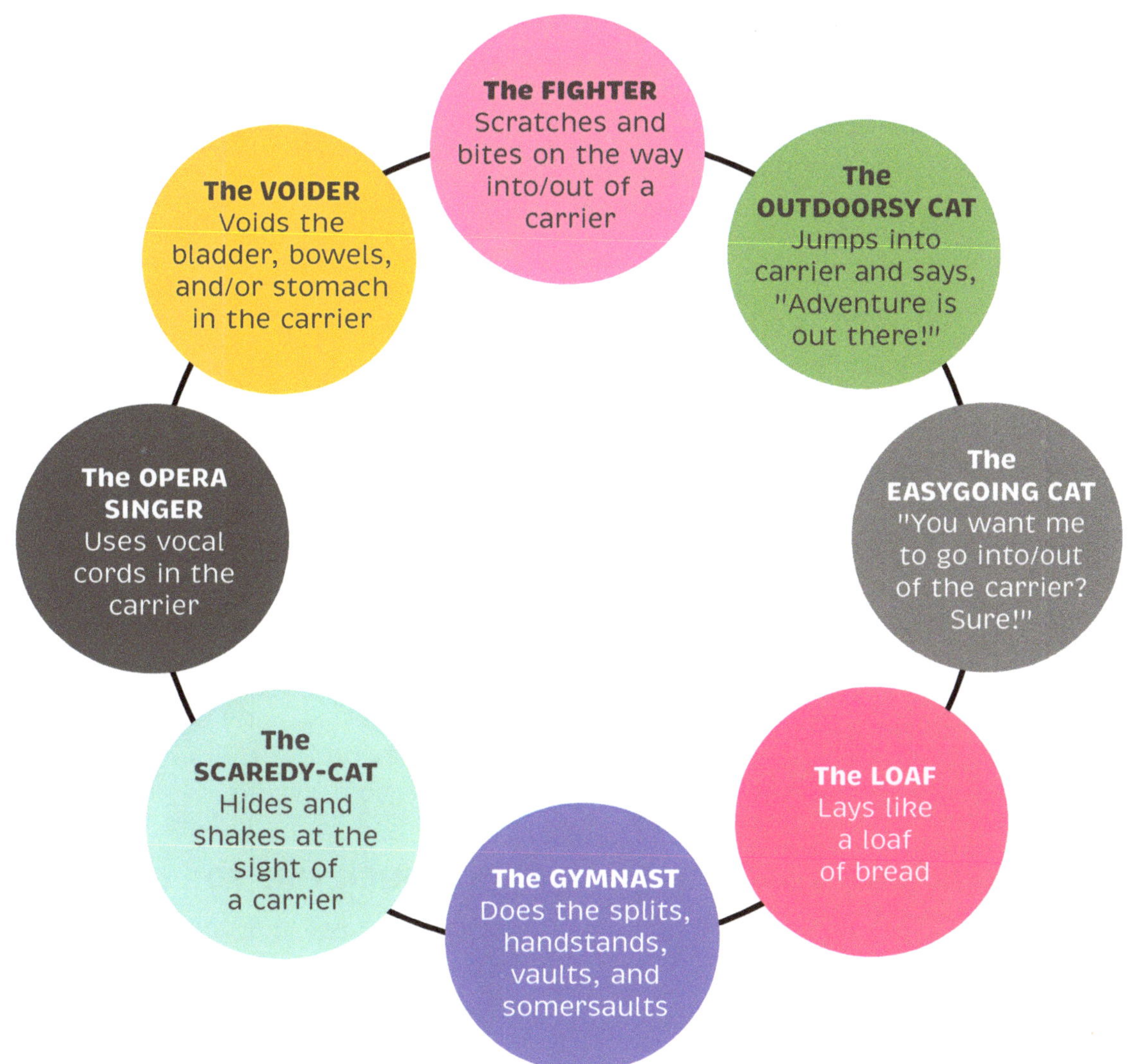

Do any of these purrsonalities sound familiar to you? The scaredy-cat is the stereotypical cat that hides. Even the sound of the carriers being taken out of storage can make some scaredy-cats hide, not just the sight of the carriers.

At the opposite end of the spectrum is the outdoorsy cat that willingly goes into a carrier to go hiking, camping, etc. The easygoing cat and the loaf are the other two purrsonalities that are easy to get into and out of carriers.

The gymnast or acrobatic cat takes work getting into and out of the carrier. The voider gives people extra work, having to clean up the mess in the carrier and clean the cat, which can stress out the already stressed cat. The opera singer tests your patience. The fighter tests your patience, bravery, and reflexes. My hope is this book will help people who have gymnasts, scaredy-cats, opera singers, voiders, and fighters.

These purrsonalities are depicted in a circle because cats can progress or regress from one type to another depending on who's handling them and what the circumstances are. For example, sick cats are more likely to act like a loaf due to lack of energy to fight or to do gymnastic exercises. Sick cats are also more likely to void in their carriers.

Some cats have multiple purrsonalities. A cat can be a voider and an opera singer, yowling, puking, pooping, and peeing in the carrier.

Cats can behave differently at home compared to when they go out. My cat Boo, for instance, is easygoing at home but becomes a fighter at the vet clinic if he isn't given calming medications beforehand.

Additionally, cats can change their behavior depending on who's handling them. Boo is easygoing with me, but with others at home, he turns into an energetic gymnast.

You can't completely change a cat's purrsonality just like you can't change another person's personality, but there are some things you can do to help. Here are some purrsonality-specific tips:

THE GYMNAST

Gymnasts, AKA acrobats or agile cats, are hard to get into and out of carriers because they do the splits, handstands, vaults, and somersaults.

CAT CARRIER TIPS FOR GYMNASTS

- Wrap your cat in a towel (make a "purrito") to prevent your cat from doing gymnastic exercises. Towel train your cat.

- Practise putting your cat into the carrier. You can't get good at something if you only do it once a year.

- Get a carrier with more than one door or opening, especially one on top. The more doors your carrier has, the greater the chance of getting your cat into or out of the carrier.

- If you have a hard-sided carrier with only one door, put the carrier on its side with the door facing the ceiling and lower your cat in feet first.

- Reward them when they go into and out of the carrier with praise and/or their favourite treat.

- Ask your vet about calming medications such as gabapentin.

THE SCAREDY-CAT

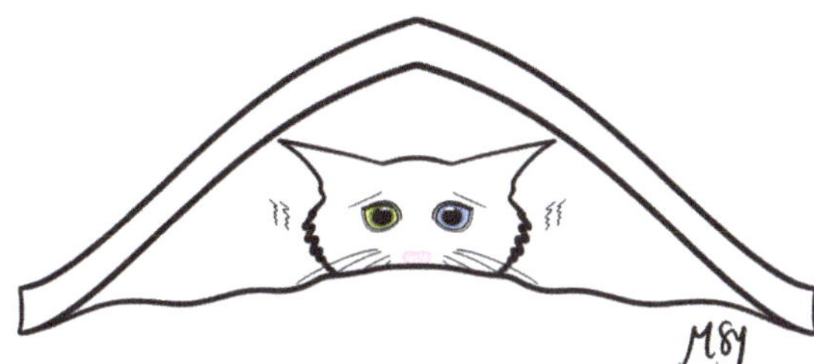

These are cats that hide and shake when they see their carrier, sometimes even when they hear it being taken out of storage. Bad experiences in the carrier, being feral or semi-feral, and lack of socialization as a kitten can all contribute to this extreme fear of cat carriers. Because of their flight response, scaredy-cats can be hard to get into and out of carriers. If their fear escalates, they can turn into fighters, voiders, opera singers, and gymnasts.

THE OPERA SINGER

Meowing, yowling, and caterwauling at the top of their lungs, these cats aren't afraid to voice their fears or dislike of being in a carrier and/or vehicle. They're not necessarily difficult to get into or out of carriers but are distracting and stressful to listen to.

CAT CARRIER TIPS FOR SCAREDY-CATS

- If you leave the carrier out all the time, the carrier will be less scary.

- Avoid using backpack carriers with big, transparent windows that can make scaredy-cats feel exposed.

- Spray the carrier with a calming cat pheromone fifteen minutes before putting your cat in the carrier.

- Cover the carrier with a towel or blanket sprayed with a calming cat pheromone.

- Carrier train your cat. See the tips on page 23.

- Reward them when they go into and out of the carrier with praise and/or their favourite treat.

- Ask your vet about calming medications such as gabapentin.

CAT CARRIER TIPS FOR OPERA SINGERS

- Don't yell or punish your cat for being vocal in the carrier. Doing so can make them even more scared of the carrier. Reward them when are being quiet in the carrier.

- Play calming music, such as classical music. Calming music for cats is available although no studies have been done on the effect of feline music in the car, only in a vet clinic setting (Hampton et al., 122). (I personally find feline music grating on my nerves. Plus my cat with normal hearing doesn't seem to even notice it.) For more info, see page 107.

- Train your cat to travel in the car. See page 109 for more info.

- Carrier train your cat. See the tips on page 23.

- Ask your vet about calming medications such as gabapentin.

These are cats that consistently vomit, defecate, and/or urinate in the carrier out of aversion or fear of the carrier, even when they're not sick. This cat purrsonality isn't difficult to get into or out of carriers, but they're more work to clean.

CAT CARRIER TIPS FOR VOIDERS

It's not just the carrier that has to be cleaned but also the cat. Wiping or bathing them stresses them out when they're already stressed.

Many people believe cats can clean themselves, but would you want your cat to lick urine, vomit, diarrhea and then lick you? Or lie on your bed with urine, vomit, diarrhea residue still on them? The cat tongue and cat saliva can only do so much. Plus there are spots your cat's tongue can't reach, especially if your cat is overweight and/or arthritic. It'd be better to prevent accidents in the cat carrier altogether.

How to avoid accidents by voiders:

- Avoid feeding your cat right before using the carrier. Not only will this prevent vomiting, but it'll also prevent defecating in the carrier.

When the stomach fills with food, a natural reflex called the gastrocolic reflex makes the colon move more; i.e., it's normal to defecate after eating.

- If your cat has a regular litter box schedule, try to schedule vet/grooming appointments and outings after your cat has used the litter box. Exceptions: medical emergencies where waiting isn't recommended or medical conditions that require a urine sample for testing.

- Use a hard-sided carrier or a coated soft-sided carrier that's easier to wipe. Alternatively, use a soft-sided or collapsible carrier that's machine washable.

- Ask your vet about anti-nausea medication if your cat vomits from motion sickness.

- Don't yell or punish your cat for voiding in the carrier. Doing so can make them even more scared of the carrier. Reward them when they don't void in the carrier.

- Clean your carrier with an enzymatic cleaner after your cat voids in the carrier. For more info on why carriers need to be cleaned and what to use to clean carriers, see pages 21, 28, and 109.

- Line the bottom of your carrier with a pee pad to absorb urine, vomit, diarrhea, etc.

- Put a towel under the pee pad for comfort and for absorbing urine, vomit, diarrhea, etc., that the pee pad doesn't catch.

- Ask your vet about calming medications such as gabapentin.

- Carrier train your cat. See the tips on page 23.

THE LOAF

The opposite of gymnasts, these cats just lie motionless like a loaf of bread when you put them into the carrier. They are easy to get into and out of carriers.

CAT CARRIER TIPS FOR LOAF CATS

Why would a cat lie like a loaf of bread, allowing you to lift them into and out of the carrier?

- They could be easygoing.
- They could be in pain. If it hurts to move, it's easier to just lie there.
- They could be scared. Instead of fight or flight, some cats freeze.
- They could be both scared and in pain.

It's important to figure out which of these scenarios applies to your cat so you can alleviate pain or fear if it's present. Can't tell? Ask your vet and check out page 108 for info on how to determine if your cat is in pain.

Positive reinforcement is also important—rewarding good behaviour in the carrier with praise and/or treats makes it more likely for the behaviour to reoccur.

THE EASYGOING CAT

Obedient cats that do what you tell them to do and are easy to get into and out of carriers.

CAT CARRIER TIPS FOR EASYGOING CATS

It's great they go in and out of the carrier when you tell them to, but they might not always cooperate. Unfortunately, sometimes all it takes is one bad experience for them to turn into scaredy-cats, fractious cats, voiders, opera singers, or gymnasts. To prevent them from having a bad experience in the carrier:

- Avoid letting them watch other cats that are fractious in their carriers as they can take on other cats' fears. ("If X is so scared in the carrier, maybe I should be too.")
- Invest in preventative care of your easygoing cat to keep them healthy and pain-free.
- Continue carrier training them so they don't forget their carrier skills.
- Use positive reinforcement. Reward them when they go in and out of the carrier obediently.

For more info on outdoorsy cats, check out pages 77 and 109.

There are cats that go hiking, camping, paddle boarding, swimming, surfing, sailing, skiing, snowshoeing, picnicking, etc. Cats with this purrsonality type are usually easy to get into and out of carriers because they're used to being in carriers and because they associate carriers with fun adventures.

CAT CARRIER TIPS FOR OUTDOORSY CATS

- Backpack carriers are the most popular type of carrier for outdoorsy cats because they are more portable.

They free up your hands to hold other things like a camera, hiking stick, ski poles, etc. Make sure your backpack is big enough for your cat to lie down comfortably in. Some backpacks are only wide enough for cats to sit in.

- Check your carrier before and after every use to make sure none of the components, such as zippers, are broken. The last thing you want is for your outdoorsy cat to escape out in the wild.

- During the off-season when you're not taking your cat outdoors, continue carrier-training them so they don't forget their carrier skills.

- Use positive reinforcement. Reward them when they go in and out of the carrier obediently.

- Avoid letting them watch other cats that are fractious in their carriers as they can take on other cats' fears. ("If X is so scared in the carrier, maybe I should be too.")

- Invest in preventative care of your outdoorsy cat to keep them healthy and pain-free.

VET'S NIGHTMARE

LAST APPOINTMENT ON FRIDAY: FRACTIOUS CAT THAT HASN'T EATEN IN 5 DAYS IN A CARRIER WITH ZIP TIES AND RUSTY SCREWS.

THE FIGHTER

This is the hardest cat purrsonality to contend with. Fractious cats can inflict serious damage on their owners and veterinary staff. Cat bites can cause abscesses, blood poisoning (septicemia), amputation of fingers, etc. Cat scratches can cause cat scratch fever. This info isn't meant to frighten you but to encourage careful handling and precautions for preventing injuries.

CAT CARRIER TIPS FOR FRACTIOUS CATS, AKA FIGHTERS

- Following your vet's instructions, give your fractious cat calming medication(s) such as gabapentin +/- trazodone two hours prior to putting your cat into the carrier. It takes time for the medication(s) to work, and they don't work as well when your fractious cat is already worked up.

- Don't yell or punish your cat for being fractious. Doing so can escalate their aggression.

- Use a hard-sided carrier with a lid that snaps on/off quickly.

- Use a carrier that doesn't have rusty screws or zip ties because the carrier might have to be taken apart to get your fractious cat out safely.

- Use a carrier that doesn't have a squeeze handle to the door or finicky zippers because the carrier needs to be closed quickly without the fractious cat swiping at the fingers closing the carrier.

- Carefully close the door of the carrier, making sure that the fractious cat's tail doesn't get crushed.

- If you can, trim your fractious cat's nails prior to putting your cat into a carrier.

- Avoid soft carriers with mesh that can trap your cat's nails.

- Avoid putting extra items in the carrier with your fractious cat because they can get in the way of handling your cat. One towel or blanket is enough.

- Use a thick towel when getting a fractious cat into or out of a carrier to protect your hands.

- Wear long sleeves to protect your arms when getting a fractious cat into or out of a carrier.

- Animal-handling gloves are also available, but be warned cats can still bite through them.

- Have your cat's favourite person help with getting them in and out of the carrier if it isn't you. Your cat is less likely to bite or scratch them.

- Carrier train your cat. See the tips on page 23. Cats are less likely to be fractious in their carriers if they've been desensitized to the carriers.

Veterinary staff, see the *Cat Carrier Tips for Vet Clinics* on page 100.

QUIZ: SHOULD YOU GET A NEW CAT CARRIER?

Is your cat too big for the carrier?

Is their fur sticking out of the carrier? Is the door too small for your cat to fit through? Is your cat only able to lie with all their legs tucked tightly underneath them inside the carrier? Please get a bigger carrier for your cat. See page 36 for more info on how to determine what size of carrier to get.

Does your carrier have zip ties?

It can't be taken apart easily if your cat won't come out of it. Plus zip ties can break. Please don't use zip ties.

Does your carrier have multiple missing screws?

Your carrier might fall apart, allowing your cat to escape. You can replace the screws, but make sure they have proper fitting threads. Please don't use zip ties.

Does your carrier have rusty screws?

If so, it can't be taken apart if your cat won't come out of it. Plus rusty screws can break.

Does your carrier have rusty zippers?

It can't be opened or closed easily.

Does your carrier have a broken zipper?

There's a high risk of your cat escaping from the carrier! Please fix the zipper or replace the carrier ASAP.

Does your carrier have a broken door?

There's a high risk of your cat escaping from the carrier! Please don't use chopsticks or sticks that can be easily broken to keep cat carrier doors in place.

Does your carrier only have one door and many screws?

It's harder to get cats into and out of carriers with only one door. Carriers with screws can't be taken apart easily to get your cat out gently. If cat carriers were designed by veterinary professionals, carriers wouldn't have any screws.

Does your carrier have a broken handle?

This makes your carrier less portable although it's still recommended to hold the carrier like a present by supporting the weight from underneath.

Did you buy your cat carrier in the 1980s or 1990s?

Since then, people have invented or designed new carriers that make it much easier to get cats in and out.

Does your carrier have urine, vomit, diarrhea, or blood that you can't clean out?

Cats don't like being dirty, not to mention the excrements or bodily fluids can be infectious.

Does your cat have a medical condition that requires frequent trips to the vet?

It's one thing to only need a carrier a couple of times a year, but it's another thing to need it every couple of months or even every week. Please make it easier and safer for your cat, yourself, and your vet clinic by investing in a well-designed carrier.

Does looking at your cat carrier give you anxiety or bad memories of your previous cat?

Your current cat can pick up on your anxiety. It isn't uncommon for people to donate their carriers when their cats pass away.

Is it extremely difficult to get your cat out of the carrier?

I recommend the type of carrier that opens like a drawer or has a slide-out insert.

Does your cat like chewing cardboard boxes?

The cardboard carrier isn't a good long-term carrier for your cat.

Do you want the cat carrier to be multifunctional?

There are soft-sided cat carriers that also function as cat beds, cat tunnels, car seats, tents, and laptop/tablet sleeves.

Do you live in an apartment with limited storage?

I recommend the collapsible cat carrier that can be folded up for storage (although it's better to leave the carrier out all the time as a cat bed to desensitize your cat).

Does your cat like going outside (but it isn't safe for them to go outside unsupervised)?

The backpack carrier will allow your cat to experience the outside world in a safer way.

Do you get anxious when strangers approach you?

The backpack carrier will attract people's attention. They'll take pictures of your cat in the backpack carrier with or without your permission. Consider a different type of carrier if strangers approaching you gives you anxiety.

Do you have shoulder/back pain that makes holding a carrier difficult?

I recommend the rolling cat carrier.

Do you have a very big or heavy cat?

I recommend the rolling cat carrier.

CAT CARRIER-RELATED ENVIRONMENTAL TIPS

Please don't get me wrong about the previous section of this book—I'm not saying everyone should discard their old carrier to buy a new one. There are enough things going into landfills and incinerators. Please don't buy new carriers just to follow trends on social media. Yes, cat backpacks look cool, but they aren't for everyone or for every cat. The large window can scare some cats.

TAKING YOUR CAT ON A PLANE

In this day and age, people fly with their cats all over the world, whether it's for a short holiday, a work trip, or a permanent move. Cats can travel on a plane in different ways: in cabin as carry-on baggage in a carrier under the seat, as checked baggage, or as cargo without the owner on the plane.

In cabin, usually only one pet is allowed per passenger, or none, depending on where you're sitting on the plane. Carry-on pets aren't allowed in the exit row, the bulkhead row with a partition or curtain and no seats in front, or the premium economy row where safe stowage of carriers isn't possible.

In cargo, carriers must be hard-sided, not collapsible, and not entirely made of wire mesh. Other requirements include "Live Animals" stickers, "This Way Up" stickers, and removal of wheels if your carrier has wheels. Two adult pets under fourteen kg can be shipped in the same carrier in cargo together. As mentioned in the FAQs section of this book (page 37), there's a risk two cats travelling in the same carrier can fight even if they're a bonded pair.

It's important for the carrier to be securely closed and unbroken, i.e., escape-proof. Pets have escaped at airports, in airport fields, and on planes, both in cabin and in cargo. Unfortunately, not all of those pets survived. For horror stories of cats escaping and getting lost while at the airport or on the plane, see pages 32 and 108.

It's also important your cat carrier is big enough for your cat to sit, stand, lie down, and turn around comfortably in. If your carrier is deemed too small, airlines can refuse your pet travel. For carrier size requirements, fees, and restrictions, check your airline's website and call them prior to flying.

Airlines can have a maximum number of pets per flight, seasonal restrictions for pets in cargo, and other requirements such as vet checks (within a certain period of time prior to flying), health certificates, vaccine certificates, and airline-specific forms.

Depending on where you're travelling to, extensive paperwork, bloodwork, vaccines, and antiparasitic medication might be required for your cat. Please don't expect your vet clinic to do all the pet export research because their job isn't to export pets. There are pet export companies whose job is to help people export pets to other countries or states.

AIRLINE-APPROVED CARRIERS

Many carriers are marketed as "airline approved," but what exactly does that mean? It means the carrier fits the structural or design requirements of most airlines or the International Air Transport Association (IATA) as a carrier for a cat or dog on the plane. Airline-approved carriers fit under the seat on most planes. There are airlines with their own size requirements for the carrier that can differ from those of the IATA, so check with the airline prior to flying. Airline staff might not measure your carrier when you check in at the airport, but some planes have such limited space under the seat that even a few extra centimeters or an inch can

Some airlines only allow soft-sided carriers in the cabin.

make your carrier too tall to fit. There are also airlines with their own official pet carriers (American Airlines, Delta, JetBlue, etc.).

TIPS FOR FLYING WITH YOUR CAT

See page 108 for more info on flying with your cat and page 40 for the history of airline-approved carriers.

- Arrive at the airport early. Check in at the airline counter with your cat, not at a kiosk.

- Put a properly fitted harness and leash on your cat to prevent your cat from escaping when you do have to take your cat out of the carrier at the airport. In the airport security area, staff will usually ask you to take your cat out of the carrier and walk through the metal detector instead of sending your cat in the carrier through the X-ray machine.

- In the weeks leading up to the flight, carrier train your cat. See the tips on page 23.

- Bring your cat's favourite toy to help alleviate stress and boredom when waiting at the gate for the plane. A laser pointer is a great option.

- Check with your vet about calming pheromones, supplements, and/or calming medications such as gabapentin—not necessarily tranquilizers—that can be used pre-flight. Even brave outdoorsy cats can get stressed by all the stimuli at the airport and on the plane (air turbulence, engine noises, beeping, strangers, etc.).

- If your cat gets motion sickness, check with your vet about anti-nausea medication that can be given pre-flight. Please don't give human medications without consulting a vet first.

- To prevent your cat from puking or pooping in the carrier, avoid giving them a large meal before the plane ride. Line your carrier with a pee pad in case accidents occur.

You successfully put your cat into a carrier. Once you reach the car, you open the carrier—don't. Please keep your cat in the carrier.

Keeping your cat in the carrier while you drive will prevent distractions such as your cat jumping on you, going under the brake pedal, stepping on the window button, or knocking things over like your hot coffee. It also helps avoid distracting other drivers. By preventing distracted driving, you can prevent car accidents that can seriously injure, or worse, kill you, your cat, and/or others on the road with you.

Here's a second reason to keep your cat in the carrier: If you let your cat out in the car, you'll have to put your cat back into the carrier when you reach your destination before you leave the car. If putting your cat into the carrier once was hard, you don't want to have to put your cat into the carrier twice. You also don't want to risk your cat escaping from the car. Remember: safety first and safety always.

A third important reason to keep your cat in the carrier while you drive is to protect them in case of a car accident or crash. When your cat is inside a closed, buckled-in carrier, they're less likely to hit the windshield or car windows if a crash occurs, especially if the carrier has passed crash testing.

Don't let your cat out of the carrier in your car. Keeping your cat in the carrier will prevent distracted driving and protect your cat if a crash occurs. Also, you don't want to put your cat into the carrier more times than necessary.

CRASH TESTING

There are pet carrier companies that do intense crash testing at the standards of child safety restraints, simulating vehicle collisions. Unfortunately, when a crash occurs, not all carriers will stay structurally sound or stay on the seat, even when buckled in, because individual components of the carrier can break, fracture, or tear. Even if the carrier stays on the seat, the pet inside can be ejected out of the sides of the fractured carrier during a crash.

Carriers that have passed crash testing come with a bigger price tag than untested products. This higher cost reflects the expenses involved in crash testing, research, and development.

There's also a non-profit American organization called the Center for Pet Safety (CPS) that does stringent crash testing on pet travel carriers, travel crates, and safety harnesses. In 2015, CPS did an independent study on carriers. They evaluated carriers claiming to provide crash protection, examined the structural integrity of those carriers, and determined the top performing carrier brand(s).

DRIVING WITH YOUR CAT

See page 108 for more info about the CPS and page 93 for examples of CPS-certified carriers.

1 Hard-sided carriers offer more crash protection than soft-sided carriers. NOT TRUE. As of 2024, five of the six CPS certified carriers were soft-sided carriers.

2 Carriers with screws are more secure than carriers without screws. NOT TRUE. As of 2024, only one of the six CPS certified carriers had screws.

3 Wire crates or cages are the safest way to travel. NOT TRUE. A 2011 study by the CPS showed serious concerns about the crashworthiness of wire crates.

TIPS FOR DRIVING WITH YOUR CAT

Tip: *Some pet companies market their carriers as car seats or car seat boosters, but for your cat's safety, I still recommend keeping them fully inside the closed carrier while driving.*

Tip: *Are you planning a long drive with your cat and worried about them eliminating in the car? Use a carrier with a built-in litter tray, place a litter tray inside an XL or extendable carrier, or bring a portable litter box to use during rest stops.*

Never leave your cat in a hot car unattended.

The temperature inside a parked car can be much warmer than the temperature outside. Plan your day accordingly. If it is absolutely necessary for you to make a stop somewhere, take your cat in the carrier with you. It could be the difference between a live cat and one dying from heatstroke. For more info, see page 109.

Strap your cat carrier in with a seat belt for added security. Many carriers have a slot or pass-through for the seat belt. If your carrier doesn't have one, securely wrap the seat belt around the carrier and buckle it.

This precaution will prevent your cat carrier from being ejected during a crash.

Avoid blasting loud music in the car while driving with your cat, unless they're deaf.

Feline hearing is much more sensitive than ours. Loud music can stress them out. For more info on the effect of music on cats, see pages 53 and 107.

To prevent your cat from vomiting or defecating in the carrier, avoid giving them a large meal before the car ride.

Avoid sharp turns, rapid accelerations, and sudden braking when driving.

Cats can get car sick.

If your cat gets car sick, ask your vet for a prescription of an anti-nausea medication, e.g., Cerenia. Please don't give medications to your cat without consulting your vet first to avoid overdoses, drug toxicities, and drug interactions.

If your cat gets overly scared or anxious in the car, ask your vet for a calming medication to give your cat before a car ride, e.g., gabapentin. Again, don't give medications to your cat without consulting your vet.

If you need to take your cat to the vet or another location on a regular basis, it's possible to desensitize your cat to car rides. You can train a cat to travel in a car. For more info, see page 109.

Once upon a time, there lived a cat with fur as black as night and eyes as bright as stars. Her name, Starry Night, was befitting. It was bestowed upon her by a human who gave her the finest things that a cat could have—toys, boxes, food, food puzzles, catnip, cat grass, cat trees, beds, scratching posts, litter boxes, water fountains, and carriers—and all the playtime, pets, cheek rubs, belly rubs, hugs, and cuddles that a cat could want. In short, she was wanting for nothing.

One day her human took her to the vet for her annual checkup. The ride to the vet clinic was uneventful. It wasn't until her wait in the reception room of the vet clinic that events started to unfold.

It was early in the days of COVID-19 when humans who didn't work at the vet clinic weren't allowed inside. Starry had to temporarily part ways with her human. Her carrier was placed on a chair where humans used to sit in the reception room.

She made standard cat observations about her surroundings. Where to hide: under the chairs where humans used to sit, under the coffee table, between the wall and the shelving units with bags of pet food, behind the computer screen. Where to jump: the counter, the shelves, the cabinets, on top of the cabinets, the ceiling panels. What could be knocked over: a vase with flowers, a clay statue of a cat, a sign that said "Spark Joy" (not that Starry could read it), a stack of clipboards, an iPad used by the human who brought Starry into the clinic, and a trash can. Possible escape routes: out the front door or the other three doors, not the closed window.

Then she observed the other occupants of the room. There was a human sitting behind the counter. She was talking on the phone and didn't seem to notice the cat carrier on the counter moving. Inside were two cats hissing and swatting at each other. It looked like the carrier was going to fall off the counter.

On the floor near the counter was another carrier. You could hear this cat from miles away if you were a cat or other animal with hearing better than a human's. This cat was wailing about being in a cat carrier.

Her wailing was interrupted by a scream in another room. The door to that room opened and out walked a human wearing a white lab coat clutching her hand. Starry recognized the scent: blood. (Her only experience of it was when she accidentally scratched her human. She had licked her human's wound to apologize for not retracting her claws faster.) In the exam room that the wounded human walked out of was a cat refusing to come out of a carrier. The cat's fur was spilling out of the carrier. It was far too small for the cat.

In an adjacent exam room was another cat refusing to go back into a carrier. The cat was doing splits and cartwheels. A human wearing scrubs was struggling to put him into the carrier. Instead of going in, the cat jumped on her head, making her scream. When she finally managed to shake him off, he ran around the room with her chasing him. Then he darted out the gap in the door, ran straight for the glass window, and hit his head.

Starry felt bad for all the cats at the vet. She didn't understand why they were having so much trouble with their cat carriers. She had slept in a cat carrier since night one of her human taking her home. She rode in a cat carrier in the car with her human to work every day. Best of all, she went on adventures with her human in a cat carrier. She wanted to tell all these cats they didn't have to fear their carriers.

THE END

GREAT OBSERVATIONS BY A CAT: A FABLE

BY DR. MANSUM YAU

"DON'T SPEND TIME BEATING ON A WALL, HOPING TO TRANSFORM IT INTO A DOOR."
–COCO CHANEL
STARRY

The doorbell rings. You ignore it because you're busy trying to get your cat into the carrier for a vet appointment.

The person knocks on the door instead.

1
"Knock, knock!"
"Who's there?"
"Fairy Godmother."
"Whose fairy godmother?"
"Your cat's fairy godmother, here to turn her carrier into a carriage."

KNOCK-KNOCK JOKE:
FAIRY GODMOTHER

2
"Knock, knock!"
"Who's there?"
"Your knight in shining armour, here to help you put your cat into the carrier."

KNOCK-KNOCK JOKE:
KNIGHT IN SHINING
ARMOUR (SIR HELPSALOT)

3
"Knock, knock!"
"Who's there?"
"Needle."
"Needle who?"
"Needle little help with your cat?"

4 A man took his cat to the vet. His hands were covered with fresh scratches. His cat kept hissing and growling in the carrier.

He said, "Keep calm, Bob. You need to see the vet today."

As he sat down in the reception room, he noticed a bad smell coming from the cat carrier. His cat had done a number one and a number two in the carrier.

"Keep calm, Bob. The vet appointment is starting soon."

The cat tried to bite and scratch the vet and the vet tech when they took him out of the carrier.

When they put him back into the carrier (after they cleaned it), he emptied his anal glands on them.

After the appointment, they had to wait in the reception room for medications to take home. His cat started to yowl in the carrier.

"Keep calm, Bob. We're going home soon."

Another person in the reception room heard them. "You're such a patient man. Bob is lucky to have you."

"I'm Bob. My cat's name is Kevin."

5 KEEP CALM AND CARRY ON.

6 5-MINUTE NEGOTIATION WITH A CAT TO GO INTO THE CARRIER

Inspired by one of my patients, Oscar.

Cat Dad: Please go in the carrier.

Oscar: Neow!

Cat Dad: I'll get you a new toy!

Oscar: Neow, I'd rather play with a bottle cap anyway.

Cat Dad: I'll get you a new cat bed.

Oscar: Neow, you can't get me into the carrier by bribing me with things.

Cat Dad: I'll give you more cheek rubs.

Oscar: Neow, it's going to take more than just cheek rubs to get me into the carrier.

Cat Dad: Okay, I'll play laser pointer with you more.

Oscar: Neow, it's just an illusion anyway.

Cat Dad: Wow, you're such a smart cat.

Oscar: Neow, you can't get me into the carrier by flattering me.

Cat Dad: What if I give you more catnip?

Oscar: I also want more food.

Cat Dad: No, the vet said you need to be on a diet.

Oscar: More food and more catnip.

Cat Dad: No. I tell you what: I'll let you sleep on my pillow instead of shooing you away.

Oscar: Neow, stop changing the subject. More treats, more food, and more catnip.

Cat Dad: You can have one of your favourite treats.

Oscar: Neow, I'll just look cute later, and you'll give me one.

Cat Dad: Buddy, can you make this easier on me, please? I'm begging you. We're going to be late for your vet appointment. They're going to make me pay a late or no-show fee.

Oscar: Fine, only because I'm tired of negotiating with you.

Cat Dad: Thanks for going in, buddy.

Oscar: I just needed a place to nap. I plan on taking another nap on your pillow when we get home.

---

7 What sport would cats excel in at the Olympics?

Gymnastics: Cats can twist, somersault, and vault out of cat carriers when people are trying to put them in.

8 What do you call a pile of cat carriers?

Some cats' worst nightmare

9 What did my cat do when I put him into a carrier?

He threw a hissy fit.

10 Letting the cat out of the bag is easier than putting it back in.

11 Being able to easily get your cat into and out of a carrier will leave you feline good.

12 If cats could talk, what would they say when you put them into a carrier?

Let *meowt*.

13 Why don't cats play in their cat carriers?

They don't want to get *carried* away.

14 What's the main reason to use a carrier?

To avoid a *catastrophe*

15 What did my cat do when I threw away my old, broken cat carrier?

My cat threw a *paw*ty.

16 How did the cat feel when she made a number two in her carrier?

She was ap*paw*led.

17 Why did the cat stop being afraid of his carrier?

He started having *paw*sitive experiences in his carrier.

18 Is there a chance my cat will stop fearing the carrier?

*Purr*haps, it's *paw*sible. This is *purr*cisely the book that can help you and your cat.

19 What kind of carrier would a cat want?
A *purr*ty, *purr*ple carrier

20 A joke for veterinary staff: One carrier said to another, "Are you having a hard time?"

"Yes, I'm screwed."

21 I tried to show my cat that carriers aren't scary. Obviously, as a human, I'm too big to fit in a cat carrier, so I only put my head in it.

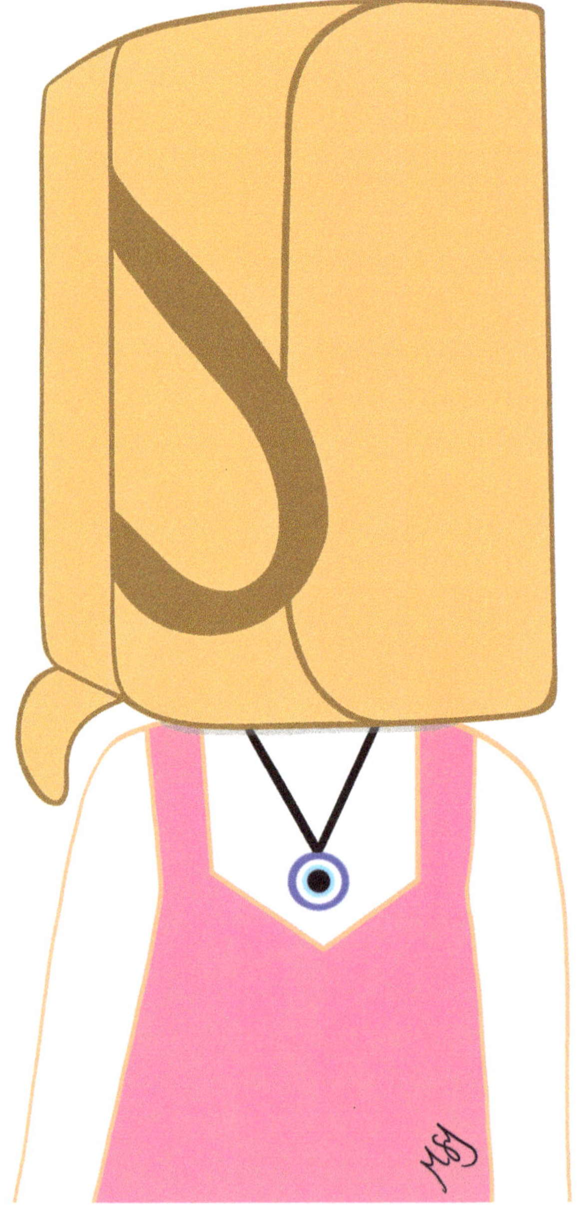

22

23

Ninety-nine cat carriers walk into a bar.
The bartender says, "We don't serve your kind here."
The cat carriers say, "No problem, we'll just carry on!"

High-tech carriers:
There are carriers with built-in fans, heating, and/or lights. See page 93 for an unsponsored list of cat carriers.

24

HUMOROUS POEMS

You probably didn't expect to see poems about cat carriers in this book, but this is no ordinary book. The British-American poet W.H. Auden once said, "Poetry is memorable speech." I want this book to be memorable, to make you think of the "ordinary" cat carrier in a whole new way.

Here are eleven humorous poems about cat carriers. Nine of them are clerihews. The clerihew is a humorous four-line poem, often with the AABB rhyme scheme and no line length or meter. Invented by the English writer Edmund Clerihew Bentley (1875-1956), the first line is usually about a person, but all of these poems are about cats:

BOO

A grey and white cat named Boo

Pretended his carrier isn't see-through

Ignored me when I called him as if it's soundproof

What a goof

BOWIE AND ROSIE

Bowie the Orange and Rosie the Grey

Were put in the same carrier for a getaway

They forgot they're best buds

Scratches and bites, drawing blood

SOMETIMES THE BEST THING YOU CAN DO FOR SOMEONE YOU LOVE IS TO GIVE THEM SPACE.

BRUNO

A mustachioed black and white cat named Bruno

Has no issues with his carrier

No Issues?! All his fellow *Felis catus*

And their parents are in disbelief and jealous!

YOU CAN DO IT!

DEWDROP AND HOPE

Dewdrop and Hope's mom is a superstar vet tech

They want you to know if you're

Having trouble with your carrier

Ask your vet clinic for help sooner rather than later

MILO II

Milo the Flame Point Ragdoll's owner

Thought she was done with the carrier

She put it away with a ladder

Only to have to climb it again soon after

Because Milo reblocked his bladder

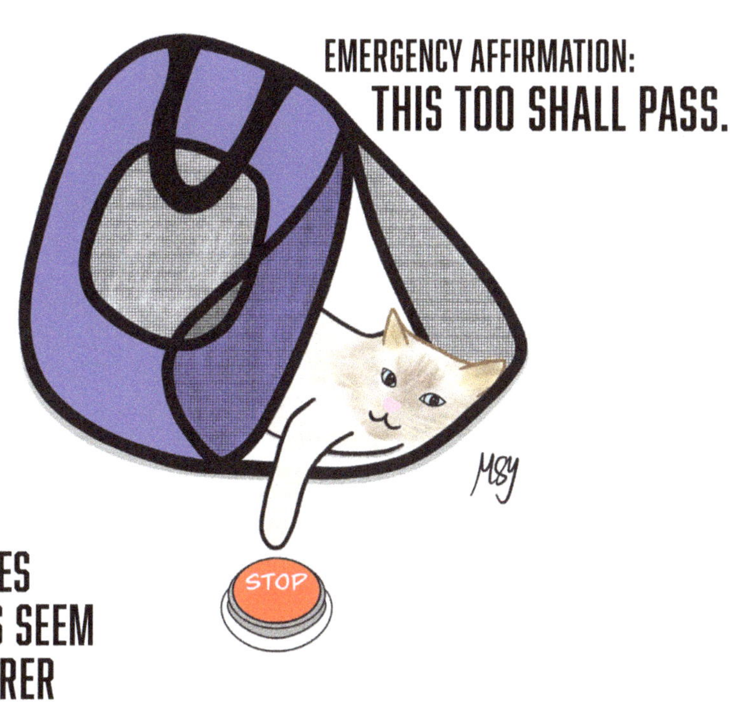

MILO I

Milo the orange tabby

Lives in a vet clinic where he

Sneaks, when nobody is watching, into

Other cats' carriers. Shoo!

PEPPER

The grey and white cat Pepper

Is a complete klutz: she fell into her carrier

She got over her embarrassment quickly and spent her

Car ride engaged in animated chatter

PIM
Inspired by Jingle Bells

Dashing through the house

To avoid a one-door open carrier

O'er the furniture he goes

Screaming all the way

The prim and proper black cat Pim

Finds his carrier and car rides grim

Making spirits dim

His manners gone away

What misery it is to ride with him

He pukes and poops on a whim!

Oh, poor prim Pim

It doesn't have to be this way

It can be fun to ride

In a four-wheel closed sleigh

Poor prim Pim

Be calm all the way

Oh what fun it is to ride

In a four-wheel closed sleigh

SCARLET THE WONDER CAT

A chimera cat named Scarlet

Turned into a gymnast

At the sight of a carrier: vaults,

Using paws for push off, somersaults

ACCIDENTS HAPPEN
(BUT DO YOUR BEST TO PREVENT THEM).

SHOOT FOR THE STARS.

VESUVIUS

There once was a cat white and black

In a yellow space backpack

You could almost hear him in space

Gabapentin made his fear erase

ZELDA

There once was a cat grey and white

Named after a princess but bites

In her carrier—use animal-handling gloves

Otherwise she rips chunks from her trueloves

ZELDA AFTER A VET APPOINTMENT

SELF-SOOTHE.

INTERVIEW WITH A CAT
(IF CATS COULD TALK)

Our cover star, Starry Night, talks about cat cartoons, cat carriers, and how she's ready for cat carriers to be seen in a whole new way.

BY STEPHANIE BROOKES AND DR. MANSUM YAU

If cats could talk, if cats could be interviewed, it'd go something like this:

It's a rainy Caturday morning. As one of Dr. Mansum Yau's cat-loving friends, I've agreed to interview Starry for her. Her living room, where the interview is taking place, is like a pet haven and library combined into one. There are baskets full of squeaky toys shaped like animals, a myriad of food puzzles, and a cat climbing wall above bookcases full of books. Her bookshelves are organized into genres: self-help, science fiction/fantasy, poetry, mystery/suspense, cookbooks, biography/memoir, and, of course, animals.

Starry shows up with an emerald-green cushion in her mouth. She jumps up onto the other side of the couch from where I'm sitting, gently sets down her cushion, fluffs it with her paws, and then makes herself comfortable.

Steph: "I talk to my cat Zelda all the time, but this is my first time interviewing a cat. Thank you for gracing the cover of this book."

Starry traces the shape of a frame around herself with her paws. "Thank you for having a long-haired black cat on the cover. Most famous cats aren't completely black. Even cartoon cats that people think are black, like Felix the Cat and Sylvester the Cat, are actually black and white."

"I can imagine it'd be hard to see the legs, whiskers, etc."

"Black cats aren't as photogenic. Also, there is, unfortunately, a belief in some Western cultures, not all cultures, that black cats are symbols of evil, death, or bad luck. Did you know there are studies that show black cats are more likely to be abandoned in shelters, less likely to be adopted, and more likely to be put down?" Starry's tail is standing straight up and curled at the end like a question mark.

"That doesn't sound fair."

"No, it's not. The phenomenon is called black cat bias. It happens in other black animals too. In dogs, it's called black-dog syndrome." (For more info on black cat bias, see page 109.)

"Couldn't you also call it prejudice?"

"Yes, an unfavourable opinion formed without knowledge, thought, or reason. Another example of prejudice is when people yell at the parents of outdoorsy cats."

"Outdoorsy cat—I've never heard of that before."

"An outdoorsy or adventure cat is a cat that accompanies humans on outdoor excursions. There are cats that go hiking, camping, paddle boarding, swimming, surfing, sailing, skiing, snowshoeing, picnicking, etc." (For more info on outdoorsy cats, see pages 56 and 109.)

Starry's eyes brighten, almost twinkle, as she talks.

"We get lots of exercise, fresh air, and attention. It's safer than letting cats roam outside unattended, where there's a risk of being hit by cars, attacked by other animals, or getting lost. Thankfully, more and more people now support supervised outdoor excursions for cats with leashes and harnesses."

"Wow, the only place I take my cat Zelda to is the vet. She hates being in a crate or carrier, and she hates being in the car. Whenever I take her to the vet, she hides. How does she know she's going to the vet? It's like she's a mind reader."

"Does the cat carrier only come out for vet visits? It probably smells like the vet's office and if your cat vomited or did a number one or two in it . . ." Starry crinkles her pink nose.

"Good point—cats do have a better sense of smell than humans. Is there anything else about the carrier that'd make her not like it?"

"Lots of things, not just the smell but also the feel of it: if the bottom is hard, if it's too enclosed or too small."

"We did make the mistake of trying to use the same carrier we had Zelda in as a kitten once, and she was too big. She got in it, but poor thing couldn't move. We got her a new one immediately. Just because they can get through the door doesn't mean it's comfy!"

"Exactly!"

"I know we are very gentle with Zelda, but others might not be when putting their cat into a carrier."

"Gentleness is important . . . when placing your cat in a carrier, when taking your cat out, when holding the carrier—I've seen people swing the cat carrier while walking. When you're inside a swinging carrier, it can feel like one of those scary carnival rides that swing back and forth, AKA pendulum rides."

"Wow, I never thought of it that way before . . . Going back to the topic of texture, aren't all carriers hard, though?"

"No, mine is soft like a cat bed. Cat carriers come in all sorts of materials, shapes, and sizes now. Some are multifunctional, serving as cat beds, cat tunnels, car seats, tents, backpacks, and laptop/tablet sleeves. People are still using the hard-sided cat carriers from the 1980s. Just because it hasn't fallen apart doesn't mean you should keep using it when there are options better suited for you and your cat. Curious cats like having windows to look out of (the spaceship backpacks, for example). Scaredy-cats would prefer more privacy, something more cocoon-like."

"I get it—you're saying that the type of cat carrier matters. Are there any "tools" that you can use to gently get cats in a carrier? Sometimes we have to use animal handling gloves that we got online to get Zelda in her crate because she's vicious and rips our skin off."

"She doesn't mean to hurt you. She just gets scared. Towels can help—they can prevent you from getting bitten or scratched, make the carrier more comfortable, and absorb vomit and pee in the carrier."

"Ooh, using a towel is smart. What else can help?"

"Getting your cat used to the carrier, desensitization, positive associations, and positive reinforcement . . . If your cat isn't used to the carrier, the experience can be similar to a human being kidnapped or abducted by a trusted person, shoved into a cage, and transported to a scary place without any explanation."

"I wouldn't want somebody to do that to me. Can't I just skip using a carrier?"

"No. Would you skip using a child car seat? It doesn't have to be scary, not that scary anyway. I'm not scared of my carrier. I associate it with positive things like naps and adventures."

"I'm not an outdoorsy person, though. I don't plan on turning my cat into an outdoorsy cat. What can I associate my cat carrier with that's positive?"

"Your cat's favourite food or treat," Starry says, licking her lips. "Have you tried the treats that come in squeezy tubes?"

"No, I haven't . . . One of my cats isn't food motivated, though, and yowls the whole car ride. Is there anything that can help?"

"Talk to your vet about calming medications that can be prescribed and read the rest of this book." Starry concludes the interview with a wink and a wave of her long tail.

TAKE-HOME MESSAGES

Don't swing your carrier when your cat is inside. It can feel like one of those scary carnival rides that swing back and forth.

Carrier train your cat. (See the tips on page 23.) If your cat isn't used to the carrier, the experience can be similar to a human being kidnapped by a trusted person, shoved into a cage, and transported to a scary place without any explanation.

FUN FACTS ABOUT STARRY NIGHT YAU (IN HER WORDS)

Birthday: *July 25, 2021*
I'm a Leo.

Birthplace:
Victoria, Vancouver Island, Canada
It's one of the most beautiful cities in the world.

Dream: *to be a superstar black cat*
I'd love to be featured on stickers and other fun items!

Favourite treat: *dental treats*
It's important to have healthy teeth.

Favourite toy: *feather toys*
I don't hunt real birds.

Favourite holiday: *I can't decide between Halloween and Christmas.*
I love dressing up and getting a reaction from people who don't expect cats to wear costumes. Christmas—with all the boxes—is fun too!

Favourite hobby: *paddle boarding*
My human and I have seen fish, birds, elk, moose, and beavers while paddle boarding!

Favourite place: *beach/Pacific Ocean*
I've been lucky enough to visit lots of places, but take me to the beach on the Pacific Ocean anytime!

Favourite singer:
Taylor Swift
I want to be in a music video with her.

Favourite TV show:
Planet Earth
I want to save all the endangered animals on Earth.

Favourite movie:
The Meerkats (2008)
A British wildlife fiction movie with meerkats.

Favourite book:
Adventure Cats by Laura J. Moss
The go-to guide on outdoorsy cats.

Favourite catchphrase:
Keep calm and *carry* on.

Give Starry a follow on Instagram @cartoonstarry!

INTERVIEW WITH DR. MANSUM

What better way to tell the story of how this book came to life than through an interview?

BY JOURNALIST ALISON JENKINS AND DR. MANSUM YAU

An old friend and classmate from the University of Prince Edward Island (UPEI) helped interview me during the COVID-19 pandemic. We both studied biology at UPEI and share a love for not only science but also writing and cats.

Allison went on to become a journalist with SaltWire Network on P.E.I. and the *Guardian* while I took a different path and became a vet. Alison has spent time with lots of different animals over her life—cows, sheep, and fish to name a few—but she now lives in P.E.I. with three cats: Puff, Breezy, and Eddie.

Puff is a multi-coloured long-haired princess with white socks. Puff was adopted after her first family couldn't keep her due to allergies. Puff travels in a soft-sided carrier with a fleece blanket inside. The soft carrier has mesh on all sides so she can see her humans. In winter, Alison wraps the carrier in an extra blanket.

Breezy is a large, round, yellow tabby who loves to hunt and nap. Breezy can be nervous and hides from most houseguests unless they have a dog—Breezy loves dogs! Breezy was adopted from the P.E.I. Humane Society where she was vaccinated, spayed, and microchipped before going home with Alison and Mark. Breezy rarely travels, but when she does, she has a soft-sided carrier lined with a blanket from home.

Eddie is a retired street cat. He is a senior gentleman, a grey tabby with a beige belly and black feet and toes. Eddie was rescued by an animal control officer who found him skinny, sick, and living on the street in Saint John, New Brunswick. Eddie was taken in by vets at the Fairvale Animal Hospital and nursed back to his current, purr-fect health! Eddie came home in a hard carrier with a towel inside. He is very well-behaved in his carrier, but on road trips, he prefers to wander the car and sleep under the driver's seat.

Mansum: "Thanks for telling me about your cats! I must admit Eddie wandering around in the car makes me nervous. If the driver has to brake suddenly, Eddie could get injured."

Alison: "I didn't think of that. I'll let my partner know."

Mansum: "Thanks for interviewing me about my book."

"What inspired you to write this book? Why cat carriers when there are so many other things that you could've written about instead?"

"Seeing so many cats, cat parents, and veterinary coworkers struggling with carriers over the years inspired me. There are short articles online and brochures on how to get your cat into a carrier, but I wanted to reach a wider audience in a more fun way. To my knowledge, this is the first book on cat carriers."

"Was there a particular moment or incident that sticks in your mind and made you think more info is needed for cat owners and carriers?"

"When I worked at a cat clinic, I remember waiting for appointments that never showed up because they couldn't get their cats into the carrier. The cats needed to be seen . . . There were lots of other incidents, some that I witnessed firsthand and others that I heard about from colleagues over the years that made me want to do something to help. (See the Horror Stories Section on page 31.)"

"What was the funniest thing you've ever found inside a carrier with a cat?"

"A sheet of stickers! A client wanted to give us cat stickers, but instead of handing them to us, he put them in the carrier with the cats. I still have those stickers."

"Have you ever been bitten while getting a cat into or out of a cat carrier?"

"Yes, once, I opened the door of a hard-sided carrier. The minute I put my hand into the carrier, the cat bit me with no warning. I think the cat was afraid I was going to scruff him or pull him out, neither of which I was planning to do, and neither of which is recommended for getting cats out of carriers."

"Tell me about the process of writing this book."

"It started off as a short matter-of-fact 30-something page document in 2019. After getting rejected by fifteen book agents, I was advised to lengthen the book and to package it in a way that has never been seen before. I dug deep. I went back to my roots. Before I went to vet school, I was a magazine and newspaper layout editor in high school and university. Voilà, a cutesy and witty yet practical magazine-style 117-page book!"

"Were there always cartoons in the book?"

"Yes, I've always loved cartoons. I remember going to the Cartoon Art Museum in San Francisco when I was a kid. I never imagined that, at the age of thirty-three, I'd finally have the courage and inspiration to draw my own cartoons. The original cartoons in my book were hand-drawn with erasable crayons."

"Erasable crayons?"

"Yes, erasable crayons. When I make a mistake drawing, I can erase it. Erasable crayons helped me overcome my perfectionism and allowed me to start drawing again at the age of thirty-three."

"Tell me more about the drawing process."

"Someone pointed out to me that no matter how good my crayon-drawn cartoons are, no matter how good my scanner is, it'd be better to have digitally drawn cartoons. He was right, so I transitioned from erasable crayons to an iPad. I started with an app called Adobe Sketch and later switched to an app called Procreate."

"Do you find it easier or harder drawing on an iPad?"

"There was a steep learning curve for the Procreate app. Once I got the hang of the app, it wasn't as hard. I now prefer drawing on an iPad though I still occasionally draw on paper using pastel pencils or crayons."

"Who inspired your cartoon character, Starry?"

"A friend's black cat named Polenta and a friend named Starlight. I was fascinated by the artistic style of eyes in Japanese anime as a kid. I decided to draw my own cartoon cat with big eyes that shine like stars."

"Would you say this book represents who you are as a person?"

"Yes, I'd like to think I'm a witty person. It took me a long time to get out of my shell, to heal from past traumas, and to be myself. I love starting the day with a good joke and positive affirmation."

"What was your favourite part of this book to write?"

"The poems were so much fun to write. Some of them only took fifteen minutes to write compared to some of the cartoons that took hours to draw."

"What was your least favourite part of this book to write?"

"Writing the real-life cat carrier horror stories [on page 31] made me feel sad. My hope is to prevent them for occurring."

"What was your favourite cartoon to draw?"

"The cartoon of my cat Boo grooming himself in his cat backpack. (See page 23.)"

"What was your least favourite cartoon to draw?"

"I'd rather not say. All I can say is it challenged the perfectionist in me. I had to remind myself 'perfect is the enemy of the good.'"

"Yes, nothing is perfect. Nobody is perfect. No cat is perfect, but they sure can make our lives better."

LET'S BREAK STEREOTYPES.

POLENTA, THE REAL-LIFE CAT THAT INSPIRED STARRY

FUN FACTS ABOUT DR. MANSUM YAU [IN HER WORDS]

Favourite type of cat carrier: *the type with a drawer-like bottom or a slide-out insert (pictured on the bio page and on the back cover)*
They're easier for getting cats out.

Why I became a vet: *to help animals and to help people help their animals*
Also, animals make me happy.

Dream: *to help many cats around the world*
Please help me spread the word about this book, and let's make a difference together.

What I'd be if I weren't a vet: *a journalist*
Because I enjoy writing, my back-up plan was to apply to journalism school if I didn't get into vet school.

Star sign: *Libra*
I value harmony, justice, and art.

Most hilarious adventure with Boo:
One time I went hiking with my cat Boo, my dog Penny, and a friend in Horseshoe Canyon in Drumheller, Alberta, Canada. I was fully prepared to carry Boo in my backpack, but he refused to stay in it, preferring to walk on his leash. Near the end of the hike, he came to an abrupt stop. I picked him up to carry him, thinking he was tired. It turned out he stopped to pee, and I got it on me. All I could smell was cat pee on the drive home even after a change of clothes.

Favourite treat: *macarons*
I took a macaron baking class. They're hard to make.

Favourite holiday: *Halloween*
I like dressing up my pets.

Favourite hobby: *It's a tie between drawing and joke writing.*
Drawing uplifts me, but making people laugh is an incredible feeling.

Favourite place: *Haida Gwaii*
I've been lucky enough to visit many places, but Haida Gwaii, the territory of the Haida Nation off the north coast of British Columbia, Canada, is incredibly special and worth visiting if you get the chance.

Favourite singer: *Taylor Swift*
I want to be in her squad.

Favourite TV show: *Elementary* **starring Lucy Liu and Jonny Lee Miller**
I love mysteries. Being a vet is like being a detective, piecing together clues to determine what's making an animal sick.

Favourite movie: *Up (2009)*
"Adventure is out there!"

Favourite book: *The Midnight Library* **by Matt Haig**
"The Only Way to Learn Is to Live" is the most memorable chapter.

Favourite catchphrase:
Catch you later!

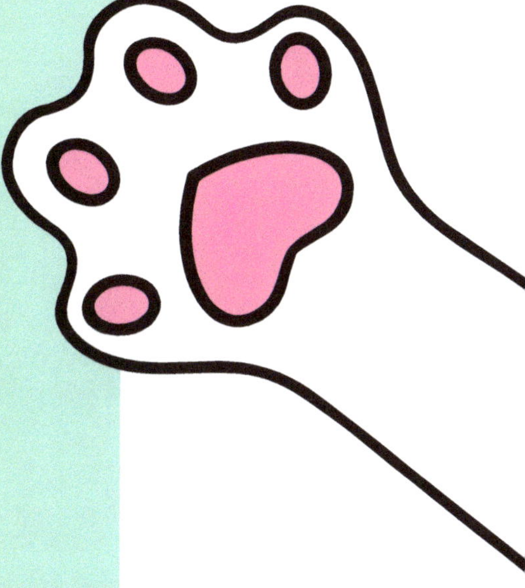

TAKE A DEEP BREATH.

Does your heart start racing when you think about putting your cat into a carrier? Do you start sweating, or worse, lose sleep over the impending task? Cats can pick up on their people's fear, anxiety, and stress, so it's important to be calm before you attempt to put your cat into a carrier. One scientifically proven way to destress is to meditate:

YOU'RE AT ONE WITH THE CAT CARRIER:
A MEDITATION

Have a seat in your favourite place at home.

Close your eyes.

Drop your shoulders.

Lean your head back.

Loosen your jaw.

Plant your feet on the ground or cross your legs.

Open your hands. Place them on your lap palm up.

Take a deep breath in through your nose. Breathe in oxygen, courage, and composure.

Hold.

Breathe out gradually through your mouth. Breathe out carbon dioxide, fear, and frustration.

Hold.

Breathe in.

Hold. Remind yourself that you're trying to help your cat. A cat carrier is like a child car seat.

Breathe out.

Breathe in.

Hold. Remind yourself you aren't trying to hurt your cat.

Breathe out.

Breathe in.

Hold. Remind yourself that you can do it. You can get your cat into the carrier safely.

Breathe out.

Breathe in.

Hold. Picture your cat sitting calmly inside the carrier.

Breathe out.

Breathe in.

Hold. Remind yourself that you're at one with the cat carrier.

Breathe out.

Breathe in.

Hold.

Breathe out.

Wiggle your fingers and toes.

Lean back if you're hunching forward again.

Drop your shoulders if you're holding tension in your shoulders again.

Pretend to yawn if you're clenching your jaw again.

Stretch your arms as if you just woke up from a restful night of sleep or a nap.

Open your eyes.

If your heart is still racing, your muscles are still tense, or your breaths are still short and irregular, repeat this meditation. You can play instrumental music or nature sounds in the background to help.

Approach your cat unhurriedly and place your cat in the carrier following the tips in the How to Get Your Cat Into a Carrier section on page 24.

HOROSCOPES

Whether you're a regular horoscope reader or someone who only reads it if there's nothing else to read, here are some wise words to heed for all twelve of the star signs:

Aries (March 21 – April 19)

Keep your cool today if your cat won't go into the carrier. It might help to reread parts of this book.

Taurus (April 20 – May 20)

Remember your cat can pick up on your stress. Pamper yourself and relax before you use a carrier to take your cat to the vet.

Gemini (May 21 – June 20)

Your ability to land on your feet is needed by others who aren't as sure-footed.

Cancer (June 21 – July 22)

Speak up if your intuition is telling you something is wrong with your cat. Get your cat checked by a vet. Cats can hide pain or illness until it's too severe to hide.

Leo (July 23 – August 22)

Unless your cat is having an emergency, it's okay to take some time to make decisions regarding your cat's health. A reactionary, split-second decision might not be the best decision for your cat.

Virgo (August 23 – September 22)

No cat is perfect, just like no human is. Focus on the good your cat brings into your life. Your home wouldn't feel the same without your cat.

Libra (September 23 – October 22)

Even if things aren't in harmony today, try to follow through with your plans, whether it's carrier training your cat or calling your vet to have a difficult conversation. You've got this! Positive self-talk can go a long way.

Scorpio (October 23 – November 21)

If you need help with your cat, ask. Self-sufficiency can be a wall keeping out friends, family members, and veterinary professionals who can help.

Sagittarius (November 22 – December 21)

If people are going to talk about you and your cat, give them something good to talk about.

Capricorn (December 22 – January 19)

Try not to be so hard on yourself and your cat today. Everyone has off days.

Aquarius (January 20 – February 18)

Need a new way to express your love for cats? How about through your cat carrier? Does it show the world who you are when you take it out, or does it look like a generic carrier?

Pisces (February 19 - March 20)

If you're not sure whether you're wearing rose-coloured glasses when it comes to your cat, ask your vet for an objective take on your cat's health or behaviour. It's better to address an issue earlier rather than later because issues can go downhill quickly with cats.

(Answer key on page 90; no spaces or symbols in answers)

DOWN:

1. what to cover a carrier with
2. recycled component of eco-friendly carriers
5. profession of the person who invented the first airline-approved pet carrier in the US
9. where you might be able to get cat carriers
11. hormone-like substance that affects the behaviour, emotions, and interactions of animals when smelled
12. reflex that increases motility in the colon when the stomach stretches with food

ACROSS:

3. what to use for cleaning cat urine
4. rewarding good behaviour
6. can be chewed
7. distinguishing features of rolling carriers
8. shape of antique or vintage cat carriers
10. most common type of cat carrier in popular media
13. calming medication or pre-visit pharmaceutical
14. what some antique or vintage cat carriers were made of

TEST YOUR CAT CARRIER KNOWLEDGE

LET'S SEE HOW MUCH YOU LEARNED FROM THIS BOOK!

THE ANSWERS ARE AT THE BOTTOM OF THE NEXT PAGE. AWARD YOURSELF 1 POINT FOR EACH CORRECT ANSWER!

YOUR SCORE: ___ /10

1. Who can you ask for help getting a cat into a carrier?
   A. Your vet
   B. Your cat's favourite person
   C. A and B
   D. The mailman
   E. Your kid

2. What can you put in a cat carrier?
   A. Your clothes
   B. Towel
   C. Toys
   D. Treats
   E. All of the above

3. What do you not want your cat to do in the carrier?
   A. Eat
   B. Eliminate
   C. Nap
   D. Play
   E. Watch the scenery outside

4. What household item can you use if your carrier breaks when you have to take your cat out of the house ASAP?
   A. A closed cardboard box with breathing holes, no slits through which the cat can scratch people, and a fully taped bottom
   B. A pillowcase
   C. A laundry hamper with a blanket bungee-corded on top
   D. A shopping bag
   E. A turkey pot

5. If your cat carrier is in storage, when should you take your cat carrier out before a vet appointment? (Note: I recommend leaving your cat carrier out all the time.)
   A. When you have to leave
   B. Never
   C. Morning of your appointment
   D. The night before
   E. Several days before

6. Where can you get a new carrier?
   A. Pet store
   B. Vet clinic
   C. Online
   D. A, B, and C
   E. Grocery store

7. Why is it recommended to hold a cardboard or hard-sided carrier like a present instead of by its handle?
   A. It looks more elegant.
   B. The handle can break off.
   C. The bottom can fall through.
   D. There's less swinging when you hold it like a present.
   E. B, C, and D

8. How do you stop your cat's legs from splaying when you're trying to put them into the carrier?
   A. Wrap your cat in a towel.
   B. Hold the legs together.
   C. A and B
   D. Tie the legs together.
   E. Ask your cat not to splay their legs.

9. What's the best way to get a cat into a carrier?
   A. Scruff your cat and place into the carrier.
   B. Wrap your cat in a towel and place into the carrier.
   C. Drop your cat into the carrier from high up.
   D. All of the above
   E. None of the above

10. What's the best way to get a cat out of a carrier?
   A. Dump your cat out of the carrier.
   B. Scruff your cat and pull out of the carrier.
   C. Take the lid off and then lift your cat out.
   D. Coax your cat out with treats.
   E. C and D

IF MULTIPLE CHOICE QUESTIONS AREN'T YOUR THING, HERE'S A TRUE/FALSE TEST INSTEAD:

1. Veterinary staff love cat carriers with screws–the more screws the better.
☐ T ☐ F

2. Veterinary staff love carriers with zip ties–the more zip ties the better.
☐ T ☐ F

3. There are carriers that can be opened like a drawer.
☐ T ☐ F

4. There are carriers that can be wheeled around like carry-on luggage.
☐ T ☐ F

5. All carriers take up a lot of space and can't be folded up.
☐ T ☐ F

6. One way to get a cat into a carrier is to use a laser pointer.
☐ T ☐ F

7. Cats have a poor sense of smell and can't smell urine in their carriers.
☐ T ☐ F

8. Giving cat treats to go into a carrier is spoiling your cat and unnecessary.
☐ T ☐ F

9. A bonded pair of adult cats will never fight if you put them into the same carrier together.
☐ T ☐ F

10. Once you buy a carrier, you should keep using it until it breaks even if the screws are rusty.
☐ T ☐ F

THE ANSWERS ARE BELOW. AWARD YOURSELF 1 POINT FOR EACH CORRECT ANSWER!

YOUR SCORE: ___ /10

ANSWERS

MULTIPLE CHOICE

1. C	2. E	3. B	4. A	5. E	6. D
7. E	8. C	9. B	10. E		

TRUE/FALSE

1. F	2. F	3. T	4. T	5. F	6. T
7. F	8. F	9. F	10. F		

YOUR SCORE

0–6: Please try again. Was your cat lying on this book, covering the important parts? If so, let your cat know you're reading the book for his or her sake.

7 and higher: Pass. Your cat will be glad you read this book!

10/10: Cat carrier connoisseur. Go spread your knowledge!

CROSSWORD KEY

DOWN:

1. what to cover a carrier with: towel

2. recycled component of eco-friendly carriers: water bottles

5. profession of the person who invented the first airline-approved pet carrier in the US: flight attendant

9. where you might be able to get cat carriers: Buy Nothing group

11. hormone-like substance that affects the behaviour, emotions, and interactions of animals when smelled: pheromone

12. reflex that increases motility in the colon when the stomach stretches with food: gastrocolic

ACROSS:

3. what to use for cleaning cat urine: enzymatic cleaner

4. rewarding good behaviour: positive reinforcement

6. can be chewed: cardboard

7. distinguishing features of rolling carriers: wheels

8. shape of antique or vintage cat carriers: letter box

10. most common type of cat carrier in popular media: hard-sided

13. calming medication or pre-visit pharmaceutical: gabapentin

14. what some antique or vintage cat carriers were made of: metal

Thank you for reading this book! Together, we cat lovers can revolutionize the way carriers are seen or at least make the carrier less stressful for cats. You (and your vet) are your cat's advocate for safety and comfort. Cats can't speak for themselves. Using a cat carrier is like using a seat belt, a helmet, and a child car seat.

Remember to use positive reinforcement, towels, a calming pheromone spray, and gabapentin if needed. Also, remember to clean your carrier and to check it for damage before and after use. If there are pieces missing, please don't use zip ties. Carriers need to be replaced when there are parts that are missing, broken, or rusty.

Choose a type of carrier that suits you and your cat's personality and needs. It'll make both your life and your cat's life easier. There are more types of carriers than just hard-sided carriers, contrary to what most TV, movies, and cartoons show.

Carriers with a slide-out insert or drawer and multiple doors, including one on top, are the easiest for getting cats in and out. If your carrier only has one door on the side, turn your carrier so the door is facing the ceiling. Then lower your cat in and close the door before setting the carrier down.

Getting a cat into and out of a carrier doesn't have to be hard. Cats don't have to hate or fear their carrier, no matter what their purrsonality type is. You know the ins and outs of cat carriers now that you've read this book! Go practise putting your cat into a carrier! And please share this book with fellow cat lovers!

Catch you later,
Dr. Mansum Yau

CONCLUSION

Channel your inner cat superhero and carrier train your feline friend! Leave the carrier out so your cat can get cozy with it and so it's ready to go in case of an emergency.

P.S. I'd love to see photos of your cat and cat carrier with my book! Please tag @drmansum and use the hashtag #catcarriertrained.

Visit my website:
www.drmansum.com

Find me on social media: **@drmansum**

Sign up for my monthly newsletter with vet tips, animal jokes, news, and much more!
www.drmansum.com/subscribe

Hire me:
For consulting, and for public speaking at pet festivals, veterinary conferences, stand-up comedy shows, etc.
drmansum@icloud.com

Like this book? I'd appreciate a review wherever you buy books because it'll help this book reach more people with cats and help more cats.

Scan this QR code and leave a review.

A PICNIC IS A STATE OF MIND AND CAN BE MADE ANYWHERE.

THE INS AND OUTS OF CAT CARRIERS

A NON-EXHAUSTIVE, UNSPONSORED LIST OF CAT CARRIERS

Listed in alphabetical order and with URLs if available online. Browse online and visit your local pet store.

Legend:

^ CPS certified: crash-test certified by the Center for Pet Safety

+ Eco-friendly carrier

~ High-tech carrier

* Multi-functional cat carrier, bed, tunnel, litter box, tent, etc.

Price range:
?: unknown
$: < Can$50
$$: Can$50 – $100
$$$: Can$100 – $200
$$$$: > Can$200

Disclaimer: The carriers listed here are not endorsed by the author. This list is provided for informational purposes only. The author has not personally tested most of these carriers. Prices may vary after publication.

DUAL-COMPARTMENT CARRIERS

HOVONO Double-Compartment Pet Carrier Backpack
($$ – $$$)

Ibiyaya Two-Tier Pet Backpack
($$$$)
www.ibiyaya.com

Pawhut 39" Soft-Sided Portable Dual Compartment Pet Carrier
(collapsible carrier that can be divided into two carriers)
($$$$)
www.pawhutstore.com

SportPet Multifunctional Carrier
(with extendable pull handle, removable wheels, removable divider, and double door) ($$$)
www.sportpet.com

SturdiBag Divided, Large
(soft-sided carrier with shoulder strap, can be converted into a single compartment carrier by zipping down the centre divider) ($$)
www.sturdiproducts.com

For dual-compartment pet strollers, see the list of strollers at the end of this section.

HARD-SIDED CARRIERS

Ferplast ATLAS OPEN carrier
(with removable top)
($$)
https://int.ferplast.com

+Moderna smart plastics carriers: Odyssey, Road Runner, and Trendy Runner
(+98% recycled plastic)
($)
www.modernaproducts.com

MPS Italian Pet Products Trasportini Avior
(?)
www.mpsitalia.it

MPS Italian Pet Products Trasportini P-Bag
(?)
www.mpsitalia.it

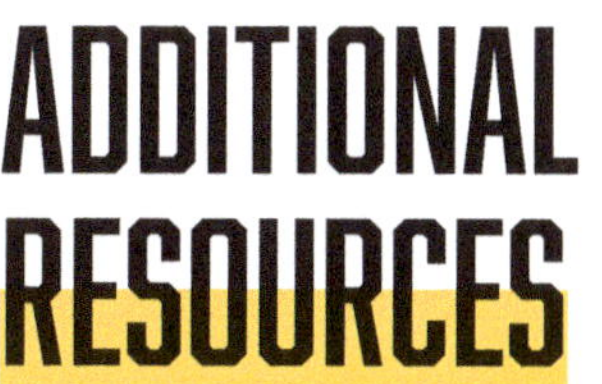

*MPS Italian Pet Products Trasportini Skudo 3 Cat Travel
(with a compartment for cat litter and a compartment for the litter scoop)
(?)
www.mpsitalia.it

Van Ness Calm Carrier with E-Z Load Drawer
($$)
www.vannesspets.com

SOFT-SIDED CARRIERS

AmazonBasics Soft-Sided Pet Travel Carrier
($)

^Away Pet Carrier
($$$$) (CPS certified)
www.awaytravel.com

^Diggs Passenger Carrier
($$$$) (CPS certified)
www.diggs.pet

*Doc & Phoebe's Sleep & Go Pet Carrier
(pet bed and carrier)
($$$)

FurryTail Pet Carrier
(with light-reflecting straps, expandable)
($$)
www.furrytail.net

+Ibiyaya Kraft Pa-purr Carrier
(made from lightweight yet tear-resistant decomposable kraft paper)
(?)
www.ibiyaya.com

JetPaws Small Pet Carrier
(official pet carrier of JetBlue Airlines)
($$)
https://shopjetblue.com

Moshiqa X Paris Hilton Loves It Cat Carrier
(with pink water-resistant fabric)
($$$$)
www.moshiqa.com

Mr. Peanut's: Gold Series Airline Compliant Pet Carrier, Gold Series Big Apple XL Size Airline Compliant Expandable Pet Carrier, Gold Series Standard Size Airline Compliant Expandable Pet Carrier regular and prints edition
(can be converted into a rolling carrier with a spinner wheelbase—see page 97)
($$$)
www.mrpeanutspetcarriers.com

*One for Pets Cozy Carrier
($$$$)
www.one4pets.com

^+Paravel Cabana Pet Carrier
(made from recycled plastic water bottles and vegan leather)
($$$$) (CPS certified)
www.tourparavel.com

^+Pawsincar Vegan Leather Pet Carriers
(made from biodegradable bamboo materials); crash-tested 3-in-1 car seat, carrier, and home pet bed; and crash-tested expandable pet carrier
($$$-$$$$) (CPS certified)
www.pawsincar.com

*Pecute Cat Carrier with Tunnel Design ($)

PETSFIT Expandable Pet Carrier
(with two side extensions)
($$)
www.petsfit.com

PETSFIT Large Capacity Lightweight Washable Soft-Sided Pet Travel Carrier
($$)
www.petsfit.com

Sherpa: American Airlines, Delta Airlines, Deluxe, Element, Essential, Everyday, Expandable, and Original Deluxe Pet Carriers
($$-$$$)
www.sherpapet.com

^*Sleepypod Mini with optional Oops Tray ($)
(pet bed and carrier)
($$$$) (CPS certified)
www.sleepypod.com

^*Sleepypod Mobile Pet Bed
(pet bed and carrier)
($$$$) (CPS certified)
www.sleepypod.com

SturdiBag Incognito Pet Carrier
($$)
www.sturdiproducts.com

SturdiBag Pro 2.0 Small, Medium, Large, Large with Heavy Mesh, XL, and XXL
(fully machine washable)
($$ – $$$)
www.sturdiproducts.com

Travel Cat "The Odyssey" Soft Cat Carrier for Every Day and Air Travel
(with slide-out mat)
($$$)
www.yourcatbackpack.com

Travel Cat "The Transpurrter"
(with a slide-out mat insert, can be used five ways: with the handle on top, as a backpack, with a long shoulder strap on the side or cross-body, or on top of a suitcase)
($$$$)
www.yourcatbackpack.com

BACKPACK CARRIERS

Ibiyaya Panorama Zipper-Free Backpack
($$$)
www.ibiyaya.com

~INSTACHEW Breezy Smart Pet Carrier
(with a built-in light and fan combo)
($$)
www.instachew.com

INSTACHEW Breezy X Zone
(the collapsible pet backpack with extra tent space)
($$)
www.instachew.com

~*INSTACHEW Trekpod Pet Carrier
(with a built-in fan and shock-absorption system, connects to an app, doubles as a USG charger for devices)
($$$)
www.instachew.com

Jackson Galaxy Convertible Cat Backpack Carrier
(can also be used as a soft-sided carrier)
($$$)
www.jacksongalaxy.com

*Kurgo Nomad Carrier Backpack
(also a tablet sleeve)
($$)
www.kurgo.com

Mr. Peanut's Monterey Series Horizontal Backpack Airline Compliant Pet Carrier
(can also be used as a soft-sided carrier)
($$)
www.mrpeanutspetcarriers.com

Mr. Peanut's Tahoe Series Expandable Backpack Pet Carrier
($$$)
www.mrpeanutspetcarriers.com

Natuvalle 6-in-1 Pet Carrier Backpack
(airline approved, collapsible, can be used as a backpack, front pack, shoulder bag, and handheld soft-sided carrier in upright or side position)
($$$)
www.natuvalle.com

PetAmi: Classic 1-Way Entry Backpack, Deluxe 2-Way Entry Backpack, Expandable 3-Way Entry Backpack, Premium 4-Way Entry Backpack, Ultimate 4-Way Entry Backpack
($$)
www.petamiusa.com

*pidan Expandable Travel Habitat Carrier
(can be turned into a tent for camping, fostering, and long hospital or vehicle stays)
($$$)
www.pidan.store

pidan Travel Window Pet Carrier Backpack
(lightweight, collapsible, side carry also possible)
($$$)
www.pidan.store

Sherpa 2-in-1 Pet Backpack & Carrier
($$$)
www.sherpapet.com

~Texsens Pet Backpack with Heating Pad for Winter Travel Outdoors
(3 heating levels, USB charge port)
($$)
www.texsens.com

Travel Cat: Argylle x Travel Cat Replica Cat Backpack, Argylle x Travel Cat "Spy" Cat Backpack
($$$)
www.yourcatbackpack.com

Travel Cat "The Fat Cat" Cat Backpack
(for larger cats)
($$$$)
www.yourcatbackpack.com

COLLAPSIBLE CARRIERS

EliteField Deluxe Soft Pet Carrier
(folds completely flat)
($$)
www.elitefieldpet.com

*FurryTail Go Glamping Foldable Cat Backpack
(waterproof, bottom can be used as a temporary litter box)
($$$)
www.furrytail.net

Halinfer Cat Carrier
($$$)
www.halinfer.com

IKEA LURVIG Pet Travel Bag
($)
www.ikea.com

*Kittyrama Cat Carrier and Hideaway
(looks like a caravan, has removable straps and an extendable awning)
($$)
www.kittyrama.com

Necoichi Portable Stress-Free Cat Cage
(not made of metal)
($$)
www.necoichi.com

Necoichi Ultralite Pop-up Cat Carrier
($)
www.necoichi.com

*Pet Fit for Life Collapsible Cat Condo
(cat house/tent/carrier with bonus litter box and bowl)
($$)
www.petfitforlife.com

*Petmate Jackson Galaxy Base Camp Hub with Solid Tunnel
($$)

*Sherpa Pet Tube Car Kennel
($$$)

^Sleepypod Air
($$$$) (CPS certified)
www.sleepypod.com

^Sleepypod Atom
($$$) (CPS certified)
www.sleepypod.com

SportPet Cat Carrier
(made of impact-resistant plastic)
($$)
www.sportpet.com

Travel Cat "The Boop Coop" Collapsible
Crate & Carrier
($$$$)
www.yourcatbackpack.com

Travel Cat "The Pack n Paw" Light &
Slim Collapsible Cat Crate & Carrier
($$$)
www.yourcatbackpack.com

CARDBOARD CARRIERS

Check with your **vet clinic.**

*BC SPCA Hide, Perch & Go boxes
(also functions as a cat bed)
($) www.spca.bc.ca

*Cosy and Dozy Chill Box Cat House
(also functions as a carrier, 2016 winner
of the Red Dot Design Award)
($) www.cosyanddozy.com

ROLLING CARRIERS

Ibiyaya Eva 4-in-1 Small Pet
Carrier-Backpack
(can be used as a rolling carrier, a soft-
sided carrier, a backpack, and a car seat)
(?)
www.ibiyaya.com

INSTACHEW Bubble Pet Carrier
(comes with a cooling mat, a fluffy
pillow, and an opaque privacy sticker)
($$$)
www.instachew.com

Katziela: Bone Cruiser, Cozy Commuter,
Hybrid Adventurer, Luxury Lorry, Luxury
Rider, Quilted Chariot, Rolling Rover
Pet Carrier
(all with removable wheels and a
telescopic handle)
($$$$)
www.katziela.com

KOPEKS Pet Carrier
(with detachable wheels)
($$)
www.mykopeks.com

Mr. Peanut's Spinner Wheelbase
(to convert Mr. Peanut's soft-sided
carriers on page 94 into rolling carriers)
($$)
www.mrpeanutspetcarriers.com

Pet Gear: I-GO2 Escort, I-GO2 Plus
Traveler, I-GO2 Sport, I-GO2 Traveler
(rolling carriers that can be backpacks)
($$-$$$)
www.petgearinc.com

Petmate Gen7Pets Black Geometric
Roller-Carrier
($$$)
www.petmate.com

PETSFIT Pet Travel Carrier with Wheels
($$$)
www.petsfit.com

~pidan Smart Pet Traveler with LED
Lights and Ventilation System
(also has shock-absorbing rollers)
($$$)
www.pidan.store

Sherpa Ultimate On Wheels Pet Carrier
($$$)
www.sherpapet.com

VEVOR Cat Carrier with Wheels
($$)
www.vevor.ca

PET STROLLERS

Gen7Pets: Jogger Pet Stroller, Monaco Pet Stroller, Promenade Pet Stroller, Regal Plus Pet Stroller
($$$-$$$$)
www.thegen7pets.com

Ibiyaya Double Decker Pet Bus
(dual-compartment stroller)
($$$$)
www.ibiyaya.com

***Ibiyaya 5-in-1 EVA Pet Carrier-Stroller Combo**
(can be used as a stroller, a rolling carrier, a soft-sided carrier, a backpack, and a car seat)
($$$$)
www.ibiyaya.com

***Ibiyaya JetPaw 3-in-1 Stroller**
(with detachable airline-approved expandable rolling carrier-backpack)
(?)
www.ibiyaya.com

***Ibiyaya NeoRider**
(can be used as a standalone carrier, stroller, or trailer)
($$$$)
www.ibiyaya.com

***Ibiyaya Travois Tri-Fold Pet System**
(stroller with a detachable carrier)
($$$$)
www.ibiyaya.com

***PawHut 3-in-1 Double Pet Stroller**
(stroller with two detachable, collapsible carriers)
($$$)
www.pawhutstore.com

***Pet Gear View 360 Stroller, Booster, and Carrier Travel System**
($$$)
www.petgearinc.com

CAT LEASHES AND HARNESSES

Argylle x Travel Cat Harness & Leash
($$)
www.yourcatbackpack.com

Kitty Holster Cat Harness
($)
www.kittyholster.com

PetSafe Come With Me Kitty Cat Harness & Bungee Leash, AKA Easy Walk Cat Harness & Lead
($)
https://intl.petsafe.net

Pupteck Pet Vest Harness
($)
www.pupteck.com

Rabbitgoo Escape Proof Cat Harness and Leash Set with Reflective Strip
($)
www.rabbitgoo.com

RC Pets Adventure Kitty Harness
($)
www.rcpets.com

Travel Cat "The Day Tripper" Perfect Adjustable H-Style Cat Harness & Bungee Leash Set
($$)
www.yourcatbackpack.com

Travel Cat "The Pathfinder" Cat Harness & Tractive GPS Device Bundle
($$$-$$$$)
www.yourcatbackpack.com

Travel Cat "The True Adventurer" Reflective Cat & Kitten Harness and Leash
($$)
www.yourcatbackpack.com

I CAN OVERCOME MY FEARS.
MSY

CAT CARRIER TIPS FOR VET CLINICS

Tip: *For fractious cats, consider having the owner or cat's favourite person help with getting them in and out of the carrier. The cat is less likely to bite or scratch them.*

Tip: *If an owner can't collect urine at home using non-absorbable litter and is transporting the cat to the vet for a urinalysis in a hard-sided carrier, it's better not to have a pee pad, towel, or blanket in the carrier that can soak up urine if the cat pees on the way to the clinic. Urine can be collected directly from the carrier in this situation.*

- Put carriers up high where most cats feel more secure, not on the floor where feet can spook them or where people can trip over them. Just make sure the carrier is far enough from the edge of the table or counter so it doesn't fall if the cat moves in the carrier.

- Label the carriers of cats dropped off for procedures or surgeries to prevent mix-ups. Writing down a description of the carrier on the drop-off sheet might not be enough because some types of carriers are very popular, e.g., black soft-sided carriers. Don't rely on labels that owners put on carriers because they might not be up to date; e.g., the previous deceased cat's name could be on the carrier instead of the current cat's name.

- Cover carriers with towels sprayed with a calming pheromone spray to help cats feel calmer.

- Don't scruff or pull cats out of carriers. Next time a hand is stuck into their carrier, they're more likely to bite and scratch as a defense mechanism.

- For fractious cats, consider having the owner or cat's favourite person help with getting them in and out of the carrier. The cat is less likely to bite or scratch them

- For fractious cats, recommend pre-visit pharmaceuticals such as gabapentin two hours prior to placement into the carrier and the night before.

Gabapentin is inexpensive and relatively safe. It also provides pain relief for cats that could be fractious due to pain. Gabapentin capsules can be given whole or opened, and the powder inside can be mixed into food. For picky eaters or cats that are difficult to pill, gabapentin can be compounded into chews or into a flavoured oral liquid. Give higher doses to large or heavy cats. (Doses aren't included in this book for safety reasons.)

If gabapentin isn't enough, trazodone can be given in addition to gabapentin two hours prior to leaving the house. Other pre-visit pharmaceuticals include alprazolam and acepromazine. For more info, see page 108.

ADDITIONAL RESOURCES ON CAT CARRIERS AVAILABLE FROM:

AAHA
www.aaha.org

CATalyst Council
www.catalystcouncil.org

Cat Friendly Homes
https://catfriendly.com

International Society of Feline Medicine (ISFM), the veterinary division of International Cat Care
www.icatcare.org

Veterinary Partner powered by Veterinary Information Network (VIN)
www.veterinarypartner.com

WHAT TO KEEP READILY ACCESSIBLE IN EACH EXAM ROOM AND TREATMENT ROOM TO HELP GET CATS INTO AND OUT OF CAT CARRIERS:

☐ **Dog nail trimmers**
(Not the guillotine type)
These come in handy when you need to cut zip ties off!

☐ **Extra zip ties**
If a cat won't come out of a carrier with zip ties and you need to take the carrier apart to get the cat out gently and safely, cut them off with dog nail trimmers or scissors. After you reassemble the carrier, replace the ones you cut off with new ones to ensure the cat can't escape. Then talk to the owner about replacing the cat carrier.

☐ **Extra clips, pegs, and screws**
To replace missing ones. Make sure the screws have proper fitting threads, otherwise you risk the chance of the bottom of the carrier falling out from under.

☐ **Screwdriver**
To help take off the lids of specific hard-sided carriers.

☐ **Towels**
To protect your hands from bites and scratches when taking out or putting in fractious cats, to cover cat carriers with, and to soak up urine, vomit, diarrhea, blood, and/or anal gland secretions.

☐ **Calming pheromone spray**
To spray on towels for a calming effect on cats.

☐ **Bonus: Pee pads**
To line the bottom of carriers for cats with vomiting, diarrhea, or urinary issues if the carrier didn't already come with a pee pad, towel, and/or blanket.

OTHER THINGS TO KEEP IN STOCK:

☐ **Cardboard carriers**
An inexpensive option for those who didn't bring a carrier to the vet or those with a broken carrier needing to be replaced.

☐ **Carriers for sale**
Well-designed carriers that are easy to get cats into and out of for those who want a long-term option for transporting their cats.

☐ **Loaner carriers**
These can be carriers that people donated. They can be borrowed by those who didn't bring a carrier to the vet or by those with a broken carrier.

☐ **Handouts** that explain why cat carriers need to be used, for people who show up without one (see page 104).

REASONS TO BE CAT CARRIER ADVOCATES

See tips for fractious cats on page 57.

- **Cat safety:**
  We don't want our feline patients to escape, to get lost, or to get hit by cars outside the vet clinic.

- **Human safety:**
  We don't want veterinary staff or cat owners to get bitten or scratched by cats.

- **Cat well-being:**
  We want our feline patients to be happy, calm, and relaxed in their carriers.

- **Fewer late appointments, no-show appointments, and cancellations:**
  We want our feline patients to get prompt veterinary care when they're ill or injured. When people aren't able to get their cats into their carriers, they show up late to the vet or not at all.

- **Fewer cat carrier horror stories, more success stories:**
  There's a disproportionate number of horror stories (pages 31-33) compared to success stories (page 35).

- **Increased veterinary care for cats:**
  More cats will get regular checkups if owners find it easier to get them into their carriers (Bayer HealthCare 2012).

- **Bridging the gap:**
  There's a disconnect between carrier design and practical use. Pet companies may not consider how challenging it can be for us to get cats in and out of carriers.

- **Role in society:**
  As veterinary professionals, we're responsible for guiding the public in their pets' care.

HORROR STORY

A vet clinic employee fell and broke her hip after tripping on cat carriers that had been placed in an unsafe location. **Place carriers out of the way so they aren't tripping hazards.**

Remember to speak up for those who cannot speak for themselves. For example, if the carrier is dirty, gently remind the owner to clean it because cats prefer clean environments. (Of course, when cats soil the carrier in clinic or on the way to the clinic, help the owner clean the carrier prior to them going home.)

Explain to people why carriers with rusty screws, zip ties, twist ties, chopsticks, cracks, and other broken components aren't safe for cats.

CAT CARRIERS

Dear Cat Person,
Please bring your cat in a carrier.

Sincerely,
Your vet/groomer

Even if it's hard to get your cat into the carrier, it's important to use one to transport your cat. If you don't use a carrier, you can put your cat, yourself, other drivers in the parking lot or on the road, and your veterinary staff or groomer at risk. Please don't hand your cat over to a veterinary team member or groomer without a carrier, especially when outside in a parking lot or on the curb.

AN EXCERPT FROM THE BOOK THE INS AND OUTS OF CAT CARRIERS: A VETERINARIAN'S GUIDE TO CAT CARRIERS BY DR. MANSUM YAU

For more info, visit
www.drmansum.com
@drmansum

WHY CAT CARRIERS SHOULD BE USED:

1) To prevent your cat from escaping and getting lost, hit by a car, etc.

2) To prevent other animals from attacking your cat and vice versa

3) To provide protection during collisions

4) To prevent collisions caused by your cat distracting you while driving

5) To prevent your cat from biting or scratching your veterinary team/groomer

A cat carrier is as important as a:

1) Helmet

2) Seat belt

3) Child car seat

IN-CLINIC CAT CARRIER SURVEY
FOR CAT PARENTS

Please rate how difficult you find putting your cat into a carrier.

0---------------1---------------2---------------3---------------4---------------5
Easy peasy   Nightmare!

Please rate how difficult you find taking your cat out of a carrier at the vet.

0---------------1---------------2---------------3---------------4---------------5
Easy peasy   Nightmare!

Did you know that there are more types of cat carriers than just hard-sided or soft-sided carriers? ☐Y ☐N

Please share a cat carrier success or horror story if you have one to help other cat parents:

Your email address if you'd like to receive the results of this survey:

THANK YOU!

See the survey results on pages 9–10

ONLINE CAT CARRIER SURVEY
FOR CAT PARENTS

Please rate how hard you find getting your cat into a carrier.

0---------------1---------------2---------------3---------------4-------------5
Easy peasy   Nightmare!

See the survey results on pages 11–13

Would you take your cat to the vet more than you already do if it were easier?
☐ Y ☐ N

Did you know that there are more types of carriers than just hard-sided or soft-sided carriers?
☐ Y ☐ N

Did you know that veterinary staff dislike zip ties (AKA cable ties or zap straps) on cat carriers?
☐ Y ☐ N

Do you wish there were more resources to help you get your cat into a carrier?
☐ Y ☐ N

Did you know that veterinary staff dislike rusty screws on cat carriers?
☐ Y ☐ N

Your email address if you'd like to receive the results of this survey:

THANK YOU!

For every completed survey, 10 cents was donated to the International Society for Endangered Cats (ISEC) Canada (www.wildcatconservation.org). Survey ended July 1, 2022.

$26.70 was donated to ISEC on March 3, 2022.

To participate in future surveys about pets, please visit www.drmansum.com.

CAT CARRIER SURVEY FOR VETERINARY PROFESSIONALS

See the survey results on pages 14-15

At work, what type of carrier do you find the easiest to take cats out of?

A. Hard-sided carrier with a bottom that slides out like a drawer

B. Hard-sided carrier with a lid on top

C. Soft-sided carrier with zippers

D. Backpack

E. Other

What is one thing that you wish more cat parents knew about?

A. Gabapentin

B. No zip ties

C. No [rusty] screws

D. All of the above

E. None of the above

Please share a cat carrier success or horror story if you have one to help other cat parents:

Your email address if you'd like to receive the results of this survey:

THANK YOU!

CAT CARRIERS

Carter, Lou. "Best Cat Carrier with Wheels (for Difficult and Nervous Pets!)" *Pet Carrier Verdict,* 7 June 2018. www.petcarrierverdict.com/choose-best-cat-carrier-wheels/.

"Choosing the Perfect Cat Carrier." *Cat Friendly Homes.* www.catfriendly.com/be-a-cat-friendly-caregiver/cat-carriers/. Accessed 22 Sept. 2024.

Johnson-Bennett, Pam. "Choosing the Right Carrier Size for Your Cat." *Cat Behavior Associates.* www.catbehaviorassociates.com/choosing-the-right-carrier-size-for-your-cat/. Accessed 22 Sept. 2024.

"Kitty on the Go: Cat Backpacks Review." *CatsWillPlay,* 12 Mar. 2018. www.catswillplay.com/cat-backpacks-review/.

CARRIER TRAINING

Becker, Mikkel. "Cat Carrier Follies: How to Help Cats Learn to Love Their Carriers." *Fear Free Happy Homes,* 27 Aug. 2017. www.fearfreehappyhomes.com/cat-carrier-follies-how-to-help-cats-learn-to-love-their-carriers/.

Lombardi, Linda. "Study Shows Cat Carrier Training Reduces Stress." *Fear Free Pets.* www.fearfreepets.com/study-shows-cat-carrier-training-reduces-stress/. Accessed 22 Sept. 2024.

Pratsch, Lydia, et al. "Carrier Training Cats Reduces Stress on Transport to a Veterinary Practice." *Applied Animal Behaviour Science* 206 (Sept. 2018): 64-74. doi:10.1016/j.applanim.2018.05.025.

CALMING CAT MUSIC

Hampton, Amanda, et al. "Effects of Music on Behavior and Physiological Stress Response of Domestic Cats in a Veterinary Clinic." *Journal of Feline Medicine and Surgery* 22, no. 2 (Feb. 2020): 122-128. doi:10.1177/1098612X19828131.

McReynolds, Tony. "Music Composed Just for Cats Can Calm Them During Exams." *American Animal Hospital Association* (AAHA), 27 Feb. 2020.

CALMING CAT PHEROMONE

"What Are Cat Pheromones?" *Feliway.* www.feliway.com/ca_en/Products/What-Are-Cat-Pheromones. Accessed 22 Sept. 2024.

CALMING CAT SUPPLEMENTS

Anxitane: https://ca.virbac.com/products/behavior/anxitane-chewable-tablets

Zylkene: www.vetoquinol.ca/en/products/zylkene

PRE-VISIT PHARMACEUTICALS

"Fear Free Drug Charts." *Fear Free Pets,* 2022. www.fearfreepets.com/fear_free_drug_charts/. Accessed 22 Sept. 2024.

HOW TO DETERMINE WHETHER A CAT IS EXPERIENCING PAIN OR FEAR

"Cat Osteoarthritis Pain Checklist." *Zoetis*. www2.zoetis.ca/content/_assets/ PDF/Cat-Osteoarthritis-Pain-Checklist-Canada.pdf. Accessed 27 Sept. 2024.

"FAS Spectrum Handouts." *Fear Free Pets*. www.fearfreepets.com/fas-spectrum/. Accessed 22 Sept. 2024.

"The Feline Grimace Scale (FGS)." *Université de Montréal*, 2019. www.felinegrimacescale.com. Accessed 22 Sept. 2024.

AIR TRAVEL FOR PETS

"Air Travel." *Center for Pet Safety*. www.centerforpetsafety.org/air-travel/. Accessed 22 Sept. 2024.

"Container Requirements." *International Air Transport Association (IATA)*, Jan. 2022 (48th Edition). www.iata.org/contentassets/ b0016da92c86449f850fe9560827bbea/ pet-container-requirements.pdf.

"Flying as Checked Baggage or Cargo." *Where Is Jack?* www.whereisjack.net/ steps/checked-baggage-or-cargo/. Accessed 22 Sept. 2024.

"Sherpa Travel." Gayle Martz. www.gaylemartz.com/sherpa-bag-sherpa-travel/. Accessed 22 Sept. 2024. (Pet travel tips from Gayle Martz, creator of the Sherpa Bag Pet Carrier Line and author of *It's in the Bag* and *No Pet Left Behind*.)

"Your Pet as Carry-On Luggage." *Where Is Jack?* www.whereisjack.net/ steps/the-carry-on-option/. Accessed 22 Sept. 2024.

HORROR STORIES OF CATS ESCAPING AT THE AIRPORT OR ON THE PLANE:

Devlin, Megan. "Cat Escapes Crate and Gets Lost at Airport While Waiting for WestJet Flight." *Daily Hive*, 6 Jul. 2022. www.dailyhive.com/ vancouver/cat-lost-escapes-westjet?__ vfz=medium%3Dsharebar.

"Pets & Air Travel in the Media." *Where Is Jack?* www.whereisjack.net/ pets-air-travel-in-the-media-2/. Accessed 22 Sept. 2024.

CRASH-TEST-CERTIFIED PET TRAVEL PRODUCTS

"CPS Certified." *Center for Pet Safety*. www.centerforpetsafety.org/cps-certified/. Accessed 22 Sept. 2024.

"2015 Carrier Study Results." *Center for Pet Safety*. www.centerforpetsafety.org/ test-results/carriers/2015-carrier-study-results/. Accessed 22 Sept. 2024.

"2011 Preliminary Crate Test." *Center for Pet Safety*. www.centerforpetsafety. org/test-results/crates/2011-preliminary-crate-test/. Accessed 22 Sept. 2024.

The CPS website has videos recorded during the crash tests of different carriers that claim to provide crash protection. Content warning: Some of the videos are disturbing. The CPS doesn't use real cats or dogs during their crash tests.

DRIVING WITH YOUR CAT

"Don't Leave Your Pet in a Parked Car." *The Humane Society of the United States,* 2017. www.humanesociety.org/sites/default/files/docs/unattended-pets-hot-parked-car.pdf.

Griffin, Heather. "Never Leave Your Cat Alone in the Car." *Adventure Cats,* 3 Nov. 2016. www.adventurecats.org/gear-safety/never-leave-your-cat-in-the-car/.

"How to Train Your Cat to Travel by Car." *The Nomad Cats.* www.thenomadcats.com/how-to-train-your-cat-to-travel-by-car/. Accessed 22 Sept. 2024.

HOW TO TOWEL WRAP A CAT

"How to Towel Wrap Your Cat." *Soft Paws.* www.softpaws.com/how-to-towel-wrap-your-cat/. Accessed 22 Sept. 2024.

Moore, Arden. "Towel Wrap Your Cat in 5 Scratch-Free Steps." *Vetstreet,* 20 Feb. 2012. www.vetstreet.com/our-pet-experts/towel-wrap-your-cat-in-5-scratch-free-steps.

Stregowski, Jenna. "How to Burrito a Cat and Avoid Feline Fussiness: Techniques to Calmly Swaddle Difficult Cats." *The Spruce Pets,* 17 May 2022. www.thesprucepets.com/how-to-burrito-a-cat-5069576.

WHAT TO USE TO CLEAN CAT CARRIERS

Brister, Jacqueline and Sharon Gwaltney-Brant. "Toxic Disinfectants: What to Use and What Not to Use Around Your Pets." *Veterinary Partner,* 25 Mar. 2020. https://veterinarypartner.vin.com/doc/?id=9570378&pid=19239.

Goldstein, Laurie. "How to Remove Cat Urine: Why an Enzyme Cleaner Must Be Used." *CatCentric,* Nov. 2011. www.catcentric.org/care-and-health/removing-cat-urine/.

OUTDOORSY CATS

Adventure Cats
Moss, Laura. *Adventure Cats.* New York City: Workman Publishing, 2017. www.adventurecats.org and www.instagram.com/adventurecatsorg

KittyCatGO
www.kittycatgo.com and www.instagram.com/kittycatgoadventures

The Nomad Cats
www.thenomadcats.com and www.instagram.com/thenomadcats

BLACK CAT BIAS

Carini, Robert, et al. "Coat Color and Cat Outcomes in an Urban U.S. Shelter." *Animals* 10, no. 10 (Sept. 2020): 1720. Crossref. doi:10.3390/ ani10101720.

Hooton, Christopher. "Black Cats Being Rejected Because They Don't Look Good in Selfies, Says RSPCA." *Independent,* 30 July 2014. www.independent.co.uk/news/uk/black-cats-being-rejected-because-they-don-t-look-good-selfies-says-rspca-9637202.html.

Jones, Haylie and Christian Hart. "Black Cat Bias: Prevalence and Predictors." *Psychological Reports* 123, no. 4 (Aug. 2020): 1198-1206. doi:10.1177/0033294119844982.

Kogan, Lori, et al. "Cats in Animal Shelters: Exploring the Common Perception That Black Cats Take Longer to Adopt." *The Open Veterinary Science Journal 7* (July 2013): 18-22. doi:10.2174/1874318820130718001.

Wu, Karen. "3 Reasons People Don't Adopt Black Cats." *Psychology Today.* 25 Oct. 2020. www.psychologytoday.com/ca/blog/the-modern-heart/202010/3-reasons-people-dont-adopt-black-cats.

VETERINARY STUDY

Bayer HealthCare. *Bayer Veterinary Care Usage Study III: Feline Findings.* Bayer HealthCare, 2012. https://catvets.com/wp-content/uploads/2024/11/BayerStudy-AAFPBrakke.pdf

CARTOONS

Fakes, Nate. "Cat Rebel." *Laser Pointers, Hairballs, and Other Cat Stuff,* Nate Fakes Studio, 2017, p. 24.

Off to the Vet. Directed by Simon Tofield, Simon's Cat, 2017.

Off the Mark Cartoons by Mark Parisi:

1. Parisi, Mark. "Pet Vac." Cartoon. 20 May 2001, *Off the Mark.* www.offthemark.com/cartoon/careers-jobs/veterinarians/2001-05-20. Accessed 22 Sept. 2024.

2. Parisi, Mark. "Scratching Cat Resists Pet Carrier Arrest." Cartoon. 14 May 2019, *Off the Mark.* www.offthemark.com/cartoon/business-finance/lawyers-legal/2019-05-14. Accessed 22 Sept. 2024.

3. Parisi, Mark. "Cat Carrier Of Horror." Cartoon. 25 April 2017, *Off the Mark.* www.offthemark.com/cartoon/animals/cats/2017-04-25. Accessed 22 Sept. 2024.

4. Parisi, Mark. "Annoying Cat Games Keep Owner Young." Cartoon. 30 April 2020, *Off the Mark.* www.offthemark.com/cartoon/animals/cats/2020-04-30. Accessed 22 Sept. 2024.

5. Parisi, Mark. "Cat Owner Extreme Sports." Cartoon. 23 July 2001, *Off the Mark.* www.offthemark.com/cartoon/medical-health/medicine-drugs/2001-07-23. Accessed 22 Sept. 2024.

6. Parisi, Mark. "Cat Alien Abduction." Cartoon. 9 Oct. 1999, *Off the Mark.* www.offthemark.com/cartoon/careers-jobs/veterinarians/1999-10-09. Accessed 22 Sept. 2024.

MOVIES

Aryglle. Directed by Matthew Vaughn, Universal Pictures and Apple Original Films, 2024.

A Street Cat Named Bob. Directed by Roger Spottiswoode, Stage 6 Films, 2016. Film adaptation of the book: Bowen, James. *A Street Cat Named Bob.* Hodder & Stoughton, 2012.

Clifford the Big Red Dog. Directed by Walt Becker, Paramount Pictures, 2021.

Garfield: The Movie. Directed by Peter Hewitt, 20th Century Fox, 2004.

Miss Americana. Directed by Lana Wilson, Netflix, 2020.

Nine Lives. Directed by Barry Sonnenfeld, Fundamental Films, 2016.

The Secret Life of Pets 2. Directed by Chris Renaud, Illumination, 2019.

TV SHOWS

Trailer Park Boys. Created by Mike Clattenburg, Showcase 2001-2007 and Netflix 2014-2018.

"Ronnie's Party." *Schitt's Creek*, created by Eugene Levy and Dan Levy, season 2, episode 10, Canadian Broadcasting Corporation, 2016.

"The Not-So-Great Escape." *Fuller House*, created by Jeff Franklin, season 1, episode 4, Netflix, 2016.

"Fast Times at Bayview High." *Fuller House*, created by Jeff Franklin, season 38, episode 12, Netflix, 2017.

THE HISTORY OF CAT CARRIERS

"Gayle's Story." Gayle Martz. www.gaylemartz.com/gayles-story/. Accessed 22 Sept. 2024.

KinoAndHermes. "ALCO Pet carriers. Is there a modern equivalent?" Ask MetaFilter, MetaFilter Network Inc., 8 Oct. 2014, https://ask.metafilter.com/269696/ALCO-Pet-carriers-Is-there-a-modern-equivalent.

u/apololo420. "Cat carrier from the 1930-40s a 93-year-old client still uses. No plastic parts, just metal and leather." Reddit, 11 Feb. 2021. www.reddit.com/r/Damnthatsinteresting/comments/li2bpz/cat_carrier_from_the_193040s_a_93_year_old_client/.

Vintage 1920's Pet Carrier - Cat Traveler - Dog Crate (wicker and metal). www.etsy.com/ca/listing/859656095/vintag-1920s-pet-carrier-cat-traveler.

LIST OF CARTOON AFFIRMATIONS

LIST OF OTHER CARTOONS

NON-CARTOON

SHINE
LIKE DIAMONDS AND STARS.

ACKNOWLEDGEMENTS

Thank you to those who believed in me and this book!

A special thank you to my two biggest cheerleaders, Stephanie Brookes and Dr. Carmen Lo!

Thank you to my other cheerleaders Bryan Hansen, RVT (Registered Veterinary Technician) Rachel McCormick, Jessica Reilly, RVT Aleesha Sangara, and RVT Starlight Winter.

Thank you, Stephanie Brookes, for also interviewing my cartoon cat.

Thank you, Alison Jenkins, for interviewing me. I'm glad our science and journalism paths crossed again.

Thank you, Patti Boucher and Dr. Julie King, for giving me feedback on the original, dry version of the book. I hope you enjoy this version!

Thank you, Laura Cox, for all the writing sessions.

Thank you, RVTs Mikah Bresland and Eve Chiu, for your input on the cat carrier client handout.

Last but not least, thank you to the following people for letting me write funny poems about your cats: Joline Breen, Stephanie Brookes, Amy Dauer, Kyrie Neil, Dr. Jodie Stearns, Lauren Strange, Dr. Emma Thomson, Lykke Vermeulen, and RVT Starlight Winter.

INDEX

Dr. Mansum

Dr. Mansum Yau was born in Hong Kong, grew up in Syria and Lebanon, and graduated from the Ontario Veterinary College in Canada in 2010. When she's not helping cats, dogs, and small mammals, she's reading, writing, drawing, doing stand-up comedy, raising awareness for endangered animals, and exploring nature with her adventure cat Boo and one-eyed dog Penny. They currently live near the Pacific Ocean.

The Ins and Outs of Cat Carriers is Dr. Mansum's first non-fiction book. The next book in the series is *The Ins and Outs of Cat Litter Boxes*. Stay tuned for more insights and tips in the series!

To learn more, visit
www.drmansum.com
@drmansum

HELP MORE CATS

THANKS MEOW FOR READING MY BOOK! WANT TO HELP MORE CATS?

Spread the Word:

- Tell your local pet store and vet clinic about this book.
- Buy a copy for your local cat rescue groups and shelters.
- Gift this book to the cat lovers in your life.

Stay Connected & Learn More:

- Follow me on Instagram, Facebook, and YouTube for fun, educational pet videos! ⓞ 𝐟 ▶ @drmansum
- **Sign up for my monthly newsletter** for vet tips, animal jokes, news, and more! www.drmansum.com/subscribe
- **Visit my website** for upcoming books and events! www.drmansum.com

Work With Me:

- **Hire me** for consulting, stand-up comedy, or public speaking at your company, pet festival, or veterinary conference. Email me at drmansum@icloud.com.
- **in** Connect with me on LinkedIn: www.linkedin.com/in/drmansum.

Love this book? Help it reach more cat lovers!

I'd appreciate a 5-star review wherever you buy books! Your review helps this book reach more people and, in turn, helps more cats.

 Scan this QR code to leave a review!

9 781738 383702